THE
CHURCH'S
SOCIAL RESPONSIBILITY

THE CHURCH'S SOCIAL RESPONSIBILITY

REFLECTIONS ON EVANGELICALISM
AND SOCIAL JUSTICE

Edited by

JORDAN J. BALLOR

and

ROBERT JOUSTRA

GRAND RAPIDS · MICHIGAN

The Church's Social Responsibility: Reflections on Evangelicalism and Social Justice

Cover image: Ghost Town
Author: Peeter Viisimaa
Source: iStockPhoto, ID 10408304
Photo is used with permission.

Unless otherwise indicated, all Scripture quotations are from The ESV® Bible (The Holy Bible, English Standard Version®), copyright © 2001 by Crossway, a publishing ministry of Good News Publishers. Used by permission. All rights reserved.

ISBN: 978-1-942503-26-2

Carl F. H. Henry, "The Evaporation of Fundamentalist Humanitarianism," in *The Uneasy Conscience of Modern Fundamentalism* (1947; repr., Grand Rapids: Eerdmans, 2003), 1–11, © 1947 Wm. B. Eerdmans Publishing Company, Grand Rapids, MI. Reprinted by permission of the publisher; all rights reserved.

J. Howard Pew, "Should the Church 'Meddle' in Civil Affairs?" *The Reader's Digest*, May 1966, 49–54. Reprinted with permission from *Reader's Digest* © 1966 by The Reader's Digest Association, Inc.

Library of Congress Cataloging-in-Publication Data

The church's social responsibility : reflections on evangelicalism and social justice / edited by Jordan J. Ballor and Robert Joustra.

CHRISTIAN'S LIBRARY PRESS
*An imprint of the Acton Institute
for the Study of Religion & Liberty*
98 E. Fulton
Grand Rapids, Michigan 49503
Phone: 616.454.3080
Fax: 616.454.9454
www.clpress.com

*Cover design by Peter Ho
Interior composition by Judy Schafer*

Printed in the United States of America

CONTENTS

Part 3
PRACTICES OF RESPONSIBILITY

Part 4
THE CHURCH AND SOCIETY

Introduction

THE EVANGELICAL CHURCH'S
SOCIAL RESPONSIBILITY

Jordan J. Ballor and Robert Joustra

E vangelicals are starting to believe in institutions again—and not a moment too soon.[1] *Organized* religion, long the object of derision by authenticity-addicted millennials and prophets of the new atheism alike, is losing its boogeyman status among younger generations. Thus has begun a minor renaissance in thinking about the church, less as a gathering of hierarchy-allergic spiritualists and more as a brick and mortar institution—something with tradition and weight and history. This is the church not as catchphrase and metaphor for likeminded people who love Jesus, but the church as an inheritance, as spiritual and cultural lifeblood, as common practice and belief—as community.

This minor (and it is minor) resurgence of thinking about the church as an institution again is part of the reason for this edited collection. It has long been the conviction of Christian social thought that the church has a social responsibility. In earlier generations, at least among mainline and evangelical Christians, that responsibility was obvious. The church ran schools. It ran hospitals. It ran soup kitchens and homeless shelters. It spoke

---

1. See the special issue of *Comment* magazine and James K. A. Smith's editorial, "We Believe in Institutions," *Comment*, Fall 2013, https://www.cardus.ca/comment/article/4039/editorial-we-believe-in-institutions/.

with weight and power about international and local issues. However, as Kevin N. Flatt writes in his epilogue, those days are long gone, even as many of those churches are long gone. The decline in organized religion is real; the dominant influence of organized religion in North America has long collapsed and is by now part of the cultural overgrowth of postmodern society.

Consequently, what voice should the church have today in North America, what should it speak about, and who speaks for it? These are the questions that bind this little volume together.

This introduction is designed to orient us by talking about *why* the institutional church is so powerful and why it matters so much. It also goes one distinguishing step further than other now-common books about why the church matters for public life: it asks not just *why* the church matters but *how* it matters and *who* speaks for this thing called the church. Our argument assumes that the church, indeed, has a social responsibility. The issue, then, becomes how the church shapes and responds to that responsibility.

This is the reason a theologian and a social scientist have edited this volume. The first part of this introduction is an orientation to our social and political context, to this nascent emphasis on institutions that we perceive to be afoot. It is a practical piece about why institutions, denominations, and congregational churches matter.

The second part is probably the more important. Rediscovering institutions is important, but the real work is not merely loving institutions but, as Jonathan Chaplin has put it, loving *faithful* institutions.[2] Habits make virtue and institutions make change, but habits also make vice, and institutions can also produce profound and perverse pathology. The *theology*, then, in the full and unapologetic meaning of the term, of the church, and of its voice and social responsibility, is at the heart of this volume. We may neglect it and still seize a semblance of cultural power, but without a vigorous theology of the church and culture, that

---

2. Jonathan Chaplin, "Loving Faithful Institutions: Building Blocks of a Just Global Society," *Comment*, Fall 2011, https://www.cardus.ca/comment/article/2904/loving-faithful-institutions-building-blocks-of-a-just-global-society/.

power will ultimately be futile and meaningless—a chasing after the wind.

The Embarrassment of Power

Evangelicals, and Christians generally, in North America are recovering from an *embarrassment of power* that Simon Schama describes. In his 1987 classic, *The Embarrassment of Riches*, Schama argued that Dutch Protestants were so scandalized by the luxurious wealth they had generated during the Dutch ascent to power (1570–1670) that large-scale religious philanthropy became a kind of valve to relieve their guilt and shame. The metaphor is instructive because as Christian people and churches amass the "things of this world" in striking and unsettling quantities, we are left with the problem of what to do with it all. Perhaps more to the point, we are also left with the *a priori* question as to whether we have made a big mistake by getting all those things in the first place.

The long walk back from the anti-institutionalism of late twentieth-century religion has been a fascinating study of just this kind of embarrassment. But the embarrassment of power, and the many failings from it that the church in North America has on its record (as discussed, for example, in Mike Hogeterp's essay in this volume) is now being channeled into a new kind of embarrassment: silence. This is fueling a new generation's focus on speaking with the voice of the church to the embarrassing and, at times, even church-incriminating social issues of our day, which is at least one reason for this fledgling renaissance of the church in public life.

The larger reason for this movement, however, is that the odds were always on the institutionalists' side. Private spirituality and personalized faith lack the glue that makes traditions last. Among the most significant factors for faith formation in young adults is not only belief but also believing communities.[3] According to

---

3. Christian Smith, *Souls in Transition: The Religious and Spiritual Lives of Emerging Adults* (New York: Oxford University Press, 2009). See also Christian Smith, *To Flourish or Destruct: A Personalist Theory of Human Goods, Motivations, Failure, and Evil* (Chicago: University of Chicago Press, 2015).

Aristotle, habits make virtue, which is true, but Aquinas adeptly added that communal habits make sustainable and often world-changing virtue. This was hardly a startling revelation to the monastics of Aquinas' day. Nevertheless, because of the kind of individuality and authenticity of our time, which Charles Taylor describes in *A Secular Age*, this old wisdom has become startling to us. Sociological studies on religious radicalization during the time since 9/11 have shown that collective habits can also produce collective pathology. Radicalization patterns in the country of Belgium, for example, show both the influence of the Internet and the influence of the Internet in creating local moral communities that build and reinforce habits and practices. Obviously, then, institutions, what James Davison Hunter calls "patterns of thought, behavior, and relationship," as well as the communities that sustain them, are not uncomplicated moral goods.[4]

Sociological insight is one of the best reasons for the greatly renewed attention being given to debates about the power of institutional religion in the North American context. Every sociologist of religion knows that if you want to track the relationship between belief and behavior you cannot simply trust a box that people check on a census form. The real link between belief and behavior usually only emerges if in addition to checking a box that corresponds to a particular religion people also attend a place of worship twice a month or more. Worship attendance is where activities such as giving patterns and volunteerism shift dramatically upward from the rest of the population.[5] Behavior is less related to belief than it is to *embedded* belief or communal belief where causal links start to become social scientifically significant.

These are the reasons that this edited volume takes as its departure point the conviction that the church (not just the gospel, or confessions, or abstract theology) matters. The church, too, is a powerful institution—we would say the *most* powerful

---

4. James Davison Hunter, "The Backdrop of Reality," *Comment*, Fall 2013, https://www.cardus.ca/comment/article/4617/the-backdrop-of-reality/.

5. See for example, Ray Pennings and Stephen Lazarus, *A Canadian Culture of Generosity: Renewing Canada's Social Architecture by Investing in the Civic Core and the "Third Sector"* (Hamilton: Cardus, 2009).

institution if we measure power in world changing and shaping. Joseph Stalin once asked: How many divisions does the pope have? He thought he had nothing to fear from the Vatican's vicar in white—a doddering old man surrounded by church mice. He was wrong.

Hence, social science tells us the church matters, and it matters as an institution, not just as a collection of beliefs. It can also tell us, as Kevin den Dulk's chapter does, how and when the church speaks and in what ways it is most influential. Some, however, might complain that a somewhat mercenary way to put the argument is that the church should speak in some ways and not in others because that is how it gains *influence*. Indeed, as James Davison Hunter points out, influence should not necessarily always be our goal.[6] There is such a thing as speaking prophetically on issues, even if nobody will listen—even, in fact, if it is a deeply unpopular, marginalizing thing to say. The ultimate test of our faithfulness is obedience rather than worldly measures of success.

A serious theology of the church and its relationship to the public square is where, apart from a serious ecclesiology, our conversation stalls. Should churches as institutes and denominations speak about abortion, or is that issue so pragmatically unpopular that we would be prudent to stay silent and work on issues that will get more traction? Why speak about abortion but not immigration, or should churches speak about both? Should churches as institutes speak on specific policies, or do we risk turning church offices into second-rate think tanks staffed with would-be pundits instead of pastors? Should we speak on principle but default on policy? Both on issues and on strategy a more protracted theological conversation is essential if we are to make sense of where the roles and responsibilities of the church as institute and the church as organism begin and end. That, perhaps, is the more essential work of this book.

---

6. James Davison Hunter, *To Change the World: The Irony, Tragedy, and Possibility of Christianity in the Late Modern World* (New York: Oxford University Press, 2010).

Evangelical Churches
and Contemporary Culture

As the foregoing considerations show, an understanding of the rise, decline, and reinvigoration of institutions in the history of the Christian West, with special attention to the role of the church in relation to worldly authority, is necessary to properly orient a discussion of the church's social responsibility today. This is particularly true when focusing on the legacy of evangelical churches in the North American context, which can lack historical self-awareness and conscious rootedness in tradition.

The era of the Protestant Reformation is often depicted as the point of rupture in the unity of the Christian West. While the rise of various confessional traditions provided alternative ways of understanding the church's institutional role in terms of worship, sacraments, and doctrine, the same basic model of the relationship between churchly confession and civil power dominated Roman Catholic and magisterial Protestant polities. Although there were diverse models of relating to those communities that did not conform to the dominant confession under a particular sovereign, the close connection between the institutional church and civil government continued to reign.

The model of Christendom as a unity of church and state institutions, in its various expressions, began to wane in preeminence as the structural bond between church and state was reformulated following the wars of religion and the rise of increasingly robust free-church movements. The revolutions of the eighteenth and nineteenth centuries in Europe and the Americas involved not only political uprisings but also the loosening, and in some cases the severing, of the marriage of church and state.

These developments demanded new ways of thinking about the church and its role in society. The Dutch Reformed theologian and politician Abraham Kuyper (1837–1920) was a seminal figure for developing his vision of a free church within a sovereign, nonconfessional state. Kuyper thus called for church and state to positively relate to one another without being wedded or conflated. According to this view, which Kuyper understood as a necessary development and improvement on the older political theories of Reformed forebears, the civil government's role is to protect the freedom of the church to develop according to its own principle and vitality rather than to coerce conformity to a particular confession. Likewise, Kuyper vigorously defended the rights of conscience both in terms of its individual grounding and its institutional expression in churches and associations from government tyranny: "The conscience marks a boundary that the state may never cross."[7]

If the church was to positively relate to the civil government in this new context, the manner of this relationship required further elaboration. It is at this point that Kuyper introduces his important distinction between the church conceived institutionally and the church conceived organically. Taking the Pauline text of Ephesians 3:17 as his inspiration, particularly the apostle's desire that the church might be "rooted and grounded in love," Kuyper elaborates an understanding of the necessary relationship between the church rooted in the dynamic organic life of the Spirit and grounded by the institutional structure of proclamation, worship, and discipline. The two sides of this distinction must be held together in proper balance, argues Kuyper, and overemphasis on one or the other results in a truncated and flawed view of the church.

There were some, exhausted from the close connection between church and state characteristic of Christendom, who merely wanted the church in its spontaneous, living expression without the strictures and structures of institutionalization. The exhaustion from the culture wars in North America has had a similar effect, leading many to desire spirituality without the trappings of formal religion. Others, notes Kuyper, denounce such pietism and spiritualism and emphasize instead formal and external adherence to creeds and codes of confession and conduct. By contrast, we must have an appreciation for and proper understanding of, says Kuyper, both the church as organism and the church as institution. The scriptural image of being "rooted and

---

7. Abraham Kuyper, *Our Program: A Christian Political Manifesto*, trans. and ed. Harry Van Dyke (Bellingham, WA: Lexham Press, 2015), 5.4.59, 69.

grounded' unites organism and institution, and where Scripture itself refuses to allow any separation, it weaves them together."[8]

It is our conviction that this Kuyperian distinction of the church as organism and institution, properly related and without absolute separation, provides an indispensable tool for coming to a proper understanding of the church's social responsibility today. The distinction can provide conceptual clarity about disputes that continually arise within and among evangelical churches about the church's role in promoting the common good. With this distinction in hand, we have the means to properly appreciate the complexity of social life in the modern world and to invigorate the church's witness and action with both the rigor of institutional authority and the vitality of conscientious action.

The distinction itself is not a simplistic solution, however, as acknowledgment of it immediately brings along practical challenges of discerning which roles and responsibilities properly attend to whom, in what contexts, and at what times. Further distinctions must be made about the timing of speaking and acting for the benefit of society. Likewise, the technique of speaking and acting is of much importance; understanding how to speak and act responsibly is as important as discerning when to do so.

This volume of collected essays, a few of which have appeared previously and many of which are new contributions, introduces and explores the challenges of the church's social responsibility from the perspective of North American evangelicalism. The first set of essays introduces the historical context of debates concerning the relationship between social justice and evangelical churches. Carl F. H. Henry's landmark 1947 book, *The Uneasy Conscience of Modern Fundamentalism*, indicted the social quietism of much of fundamentalism and introduced concern for social responsibility into modern evangelicalism. In his first chapter, reprinted here, Henry outlines his case for why there has been a disappearance, or in his words "evaporation," of fundamentalist regard for humanity and a corresponding withdrawal from

---

8. Abraham Kuyper, *Rooted & Grounded: The Church as Organism and Institution*, trans. and ed. Nelson D. Kloosterman (Grand Rapids: Christian's Library Press, 2013), 5.

social engagement. One group was notably exempted from the sharper edges of this larger critique, however. As Henry observed, "There are Fundamentalist groups, admittedly, which have not lost a keen world reference, especially those alert to their Reformational lineage in John Calvin. Their interest in ethics is demanded, rather than precluded, by their doctrinal fervor."[9] Essays by J. Howard Pew and Richard J. Mouw attest to the ongoing complexities of evangelical social engagement, while highlighting the historic Reformed, and particularly neo-Calvinistic, contributions in this regard.

The following two sections are devoted to exploring the legacy of this Reformed perspective and how it might serve to bring the church's social responsibility into sharper relief. In the section Principles of Responsibility, Jessica Driesenga, David T. Koyzis, and Michael R. Wagenman provide the theological and historical backgrounds for the Reformed understanding of the church as both organism and institution. We cannot validly contend either that the institutional church is of no significance or that it has no social responsibility. Such conclusions help inform and guide the essays included in the third section, Practices of Responsibility. Here we see in particular how different understandings of the church's institutional and organic roles can variously impact concrete proposals for Christian action.

Whereas the first three sections narrow the focus from evangelicalism more broadly to particularly Reformed contributions to the principles and practices of social responsibility, the final set of essays broadens the discussion to apply to the relationship of Christians and the church to the wider arena of social institutions. The institutional church is not the only way in which Christians are called to engage the world. We must thus also think for both today and for tomorrow about social as well as public justice promoted not only by churches but also by families and schools, civil associations and service groups, think tanks and charities, businesses and governments.

---

9. Carl F. H. Henry, *The Uneasy Conscience of Modern Fundamentalism* (Grand Rapids: Eerdmans, 1947), 18. See page 17 in this volume.

A final essay by the historian Kevin N. Flatt provides a fitting conclusion to this volume's focus on the promises and perils of the church's social responsibility. We must properly understand what it means, in Jesus' words, to "seek first the kingdom of God and his righteousness" (Matt. 6:33), and thus to properly relate and orient the concerns of his kingdom, which "is not a matter of eating and drinking but of righteousness and peace and joy in the Holy Spirit" (Rom. 14:17), to the things of this world.

Conclusion

Abraham Kuyper introduced the distinction between the church as organism and institution at a time of upheaval and transition from Christendom to a post-Christendom social order. Today we face similar changes as we live in not only post-Christendom but also in many ways increasingly post-Christian societies.[10] The same temptations that Kuyper identified in his own day in the midst of such uncertainties are seemingly valid options today: withdrawal from the broader world into ecclesially defined and delimited institutions or rejection of such institutions as outmoded and obsolete. From its beginning, evangelicalism has implicitly recognized the dangers of these alternatives, and the Reformed tradition's reflections on the nature of the church and its role in society are worth revisiting and reconsidering in light of contemporary challenges. The church, both in its institutional and its organic expressions, has social responsibility. Our challenge today remains the perennial challenge of the Christian faith: to discern what it means to faithfully follow Jesus Christ in the context of our individual and institutional realities. We hope that this volume may be an aid to that end.

---

10. On the relevance of Kuyper's views today, see Ad de Bruijne, "'Colony of Heaven': Abraham Kuyper's Ecclesiology in the Twenty-First Century," *Journal of Markets & Morality* 17, no. 2 (Fall 2014): 445–90.

PART 1

EVANGELICALISM AND SOCIAL JUSTICE

One

THE EVAPORATION
OF FUNDAMENTALIST
HUMANITARIANISM*

Carl F. H. Henry

T he present tendency of conservative Christianity is to make
much of the embarrassment of religious modernism.

The modernist embarrassment is serious indeed. The shallow
insistence on inevitable world progress and on man's essential
goodness has been violently declared false. Not only sound Bible
exegesis but the world events of 1914–1946 indict optimistic
liberalism.

But contemporary Fundamentalism is not without its own
moments of guilt. For the world crisis serves to embarrass
Fundamentalism also. The uncomfortableness of evangelicalism
cannot be palliated by an emphasis on someone else's uneasy
predicament. Even if it could, the device would hardly escape
attention from the alert modern mind.

The predicament of contemporary evangelicalism can be set
forth from two vantage points, that of the non-evangelicals and

---

* The word "humanitarianism" is used in the sense of benevolent regard
for the interests of mankind. Ed. note: This chapter used with permission here originally appeared as Carl F. H. Henry, "The Evaporation of
Fundamentalist Humanitarianism," in *The Uneasy Conscience of Modern
Fundamentalism* (1947; repr., Grand Rapids: Eerdmans, 2003), 1–11.

that of the evangelicals themselves. From whichever direction the problem is approached, it is serious enough.

Against Protestant Fundamentalism the non-evangelicals level the charge that it has no social program calling for a practical attack on acknowledged world evils. True, other complaints are made against Christian supernaturalism. Representative spokesmen for religious liberalism, for ethical idealism, for religious humanism, and for pessimism, are linked by a common network of assumptions which clearly differentiates their philosophic premises from the orthodox Hebrew-Christian view. Non-Christian groups have no dealings with a supernaturalistic metaphysics. But nonetheless—though they regard contemporary orthodoxy as a vestigial remnant of traditional obscurantism—they theoretically recognize the philosophic right of the evangelicals to hold any doctrinal framework they may desire. But what is almost wholly unintelligible to the naturalistic and idealistic groups, burdened as they are for a new world order, is the apparent lack of any social passion in Protestant Fundamentalism. On this evaluation, Fundamentalism is the modern priest and Levite, by-passing suffering humanity.

The picture is clear when one brings into focus such admitted social evils as aggressive warfare, racial hatred and intolerance, the liquor traffic, and exploitation of labor or management, whichever it may be.

The social reform movements dedicated to the elimination of such evils do not have the active, let alone vigorous, cooperation of large segments of evangelical Christianity. In fact, Fundamentalist churches increasingly have repudiated the very movements whose most energetic efforts have gone into an attack on such social ills. The studied Fundamentalist avoidance of, and bitter criticism of, the World Council of Churches and the Federal Council of Churches of Christ in America is a pertinent example.

Now, such resistance would be far more intelligible to non-evangelicals were it accompanied by an equally forceful assault on social evils in a distinctly supernaturalistic framework. But, by and large, the Fundamentalist opposition to societal ills has been more vocal than actual. Some concerted effort has been attempted through organizations like the National Association of Evangelicals or the American Council of Churches. Southern Baptists have a somewhat better record, coupled with rejection of the Federal Council. But evangelical social action has been spotty and usually of the emergency type.

The situation has even a darker side. The great majority of Fundamentalist clergymen, during the past generation of world disintegration, became increasingly less vocal about social evils. It was unusual to find a conservative preacher occupied at length with world ills.

In a company of more than one hundred representative evangelical pastors, the writer proposed the following question: "How many of you, during the past six months, have preached a sermon devoted in large part to a condemnation of such social evils as aggressive warfare, racial hatred and intolerance, the liquor traffic, exploitation of labor or management, or the like—a sermon containing not merely an incidental or illustrative reference, but directed mainly against such evils and proposing the framework in which you think solution is possible?" Not a single hand was raised in response. Now this situation is not characteristic only of one particular denominational group of Fundamentalists; rather, a predominant trait, in most Fundamentalist preaching, is this reluctance to come to grips with social evils.

There are Fundamentalist groups, admittedly, which have not lost a keen world reference, especially those alert to their Reformational lineage in John Calvin. Their interest in ethics is demanded, rather than precluded, by their doctrinal fervor. Holding fast to an ideology of supernaturalism, these groups have sometimes been tempted to dissociate themselves from the Fundamentalist camp because of the widespread notion that indifference to world evils is essential to Fundamentalism. And, after all, social irresponsibility was not the only trend that was imputed to Fundamentalist circles. Modern prejudice, justly or unjustly, had come to identify Fundamentalism largely in terms of an anti-ecumenical spirit of independent isolationism, an uncritically-held set of theological formulas,[1] an overly-emotional

---

1. Many newspapers have inaccurately applied the Fundamentalist tag to cultists (like the Mormon polygamists) whom the evangelicals would be the first to disown.

15

type of revivalism. There is also the tendency to replace great church music by a barn-dance variety of semi-religious choruses; some churches have almost become spiritualized juke boxes. It was the recognition, by the ethically alert Fundamentalist minority, that such tendencies do not express the inherent genius of the great evangelical tradition that prevented their desertion from the Fundamentalist camp. Spokesmen particularly for orthodox Reformed groups saw that the title of "Fundamentalism" was applied initially with doctrinal fidelity, rather than ethical irresponsibility, as the frame of reference. Fundamentalism was a Bible-believing Christianity which regarded the supernatural as a part of the essence of the Biblical view; the miraculous was not to be viewed, as in liberalism, as an incidental and superfluous accretion. It was from its affirmation of the historic evangelical doctrinal fundamentals that modern orthodoxy received its name, and not from its silence on pressing global problems. This was clearly seen by spokesmen for contemporary Fundamentalism like the late J. Gresham Machen, who vigorously insisted that Christianity has a message relevant to the world crisis, however staggering the issues.

The average Fundamentalist's indifference to social implications of his religious message has been so marked, however, that the non-evangelicals have sometimes classified him with the pessimist in his attitude toward world conditions.

Of all the seemingly incongruous weddings in philosophy, this is the most striking. That Christian supernaturalism, which as a matter of historical record furnished the background and in some sense the support for the modern humanisms and idealisms, should be accused of having lost its own devotion to human well-being, is indeed a startling accusation.

But, from the standpoint of not a few religious modernists, ethical idealists and humanists, the common strand that runs through Fundamentalism and pessimism is that both are viewpoints from which the humanism, or humanitarianism, has evaporated.

This is not to suggest that Fundamentalism had no militant opposition to sin. Of all modern viewpoints, when measured against the black background of human nature disclosed by the generation of two world wars, Fundamentalism provided the most realistic appraisal of the condition of man. The sinfulness of man, and the exceeding sinfulness of sin, and that God alone can save man from his disaster, are insistences that were heard with commonplace frequency only within the evangelical churches. But the sin against which Fundamentalism has inveighed, almost exclusively, was individual sin rather than social evil.

It is not fair to say that the ethical platform of all conservative churches has clustered about such platitudes as "abstain from intoxicating beverages, movies, dancing, card-playing, and smoking," but there are multitudes of Fundamentalist congregations in which these are the main points of reference for ethical speculation. In one of the large Christian colleges, a chapel speaker recently expressed amazement that the campus newspaper could devote so much space to the all-important problem of whether it is right to play "rook," while the nations of the world are playing with fire.

And yet it ought not to be overlooked that, in its attack on personal sins, there is an indirect coming to grips in Fundamentalist churches with some of the major contemporary problems. The bitter opposition to intoxicating beverages is, in a localized sense, an attack upon the liquor traffic, even though it does nothing to curb the menace itself and concentrates upon schooling the believer to circumvent it. Again, while the Fundamentalist's opposition to the theatre is sometimes so deep-rooted that it is forgotten that the camera may also serve to the glory of God, he nevertheless is expressing a vigorous protest against the secular and often pagan standards of value which Hollywood film producers have consistently enthroned and glorified. At this point, in fact, the Fundamentalist has often been more sensitive to the danger of undermining Christian convictions by propaganda means than has the religious modernist with his selection of "best, good, and unrecommended films." And yet, the Fundamentalist appears to pursue a rather foredoomed approach, schooling his constituency against all movies, as if they are inherently evil, so that there is no direct attempt to change the external picture itself.

The problem of personal ethics, moreover, is complicated no little by the shifting standards in various sections of the country,

17

among Fundamentalists themselves. Among evangelicals, for example, smoking is hardly considered the sin in the southern tobacco-growing states that it is in the north.[2] And the northern Baptist pastor who would join his wife for mixed public swimming would be called before his board of deacons in many a southern church.

Now, the purpose of such examples is not to promote a plea for laxity in personal morals. It is simply to emphasize that such personal issues are themselves frequently in a state of environmental flux which, if anything, adds to the predicament of the Fundamentalist pastor on the score of ethical preaching.

Even more serious is the mounting repudiation in evangelical circles of Fundamentalist standards for the practical moral life. This testifies to more than a growing estrangement from traditional ways of living. As seen by those who are not evangelicals, this movement away from the evangelical evaluation of life and duty, in the personal as well as social code of behavior, is an inevitable consequence of an ideology which refuses to relate itself to the cardinal issues of the global dilemma. The non-Christian idealists and naturalists know, of course, that their outlooks demand an evaluation of life which differs from the Fundamental appraisal, but they trace the growing Fundamentalist revolt against stringent personal prohibitions, to the peculiar strategy of evangelical ethics, as much as to the penetrative dissemination of anti-Christian moral theories. It remains a question whether one can be perpetually indifferent to the problems of social justice and international order, and develop a wholesome personal ethics.

In mentioning the typical ethical insistences of Fundamentalist churches, it would be unfair not to allude to the strict attitude taken toward divorce, as contrasted with the increasingly loose secular view of family relations. The insistence that only death

---

2. Although the Southern Baptist Convention in 1937 affirmed "that the prevalence of smoking among Christian people, especially among preachers, church leaders, and denominational workers, is not only detrimental to the health of those who participate, but hurtful to the cause of Christ in that it weakens the messages and lowers the influence of those charged with the preservation and spread of the Gospel."

or adultery can sever the marriage bond is maintained nowhere today with such a conviction of absoluteness as in Fundamentalist circles, although there are here, as everywhere, exceptions. The contribution of this viewpoint to the integrity of the family, and its significance in precluding juvenile delinquency, is of no small moment in its social consequences. From a certain perspective it can be said that the effort to remedy the disintegration of the American home, pressed by social reformers, does not get at the heart of the problem as directly as the Fundamentalist proclamation of the divine sanction of a monogamous family life.

But here again it must also be conceded that the defection of American culture from a vital Christianity means that the problem of the home and of juvenile delinquency is unconfronted in countless family circles where remedial measures might create a more favorable soil for the preaching of the Gospel. By such argument even those who have disagreed with a supernaturalist ideology have sought to enlist evangelicalism in reform programs.

The failure of the evangelical movement to react favorably on any widespread front to campaigns against social evils has led, finally, to a suspicion on the part of non-evangelicals that there is something in the very nature of Fundamentalism which makes a world ethical view impossible. The conviction is widespread that Fundamentalism takes too pessimistic a view of human nature to make a social program practicable.

This modern mind-set, insisting that evangelical supernaturalism has inherent within it an ideological fault which precludes any vital social thrust, is one of the most disturbing dividing lines in contemporary thought. In the struggle for a world mind which will make global order and brotherhood a possibility, contemporary speculation has no hearing whatever for a viewpoint which it suspects has no world program. It dismisses Fundamentalism with the thought that, in this expression of the Great Tradition, the humanitarianism has evaporated from Christianity.

Two

SHOULD THE CHURCH "MEDDLE" IN CIVIL AFFAIRS?[*]

J. Howard Pew

O f all the institutions of human society, the Christian church is surely the most amazing. Standing like a rock amid the shifting currents and cultures of the ages, it has occupied a unique place in man's life for almost 2000 years. While other institutions have come and gone, political and economic systems waxed and waned, the church, alone among them all, has endured.

I have no worry that it will not continue to endure. I do worry, however, when leaders of the church show signs of jeopardizing its power and influence by taking it away from its main mission. To be specific: as an active churchman for more than 40 years, I am concerned that many of the church's top leaders today—especially in what are called the "mainstream" denominations—are sorely failing its members in two ways: (1) by succumbing to a creeping tendency to downgrade the Bible as the infallible Word of God, and (2) by efforts to shift the church's main thrust from the spiritual to the secular. The two, I believe, are related.

---

* Reprinted with permission from *The Reader's Digest*, May 1966, 49–54.

Fixed Stars

The strength of the church in the past has been its reliance upon the Bible as the basis of ultimate, eternal truth. From the time "holy men of God" spoke and wrote "as they were moved by the Holy Ghost," the Scriptures have been accepted as the one changeless guide to faith, morals and life. They were so accepted by Christ himself: "Ye do err, not knowing the Scriptures."

If there is one thing that modern man needs more than anything else, psychologists are agreed, it is fixed stars to guide him. Modern man has too few such fixed stars. The philosophy of our day makes all truth relative. Standards, values, ethics, morals—these, were are told, are subject to change according to the customs of the times.

The effect of that kind of thinking has been devastating to the morals of our times. I'm convinced that much of the jittery, uncertain mood of youth today is traceable to the lack of something firm and unchangeable to stand upon. As one brilliant but confused young man said to me recently, "The trouble is, we're being asked to play the game of life without any stable ground rules."

Said the late Richard M. Weaver, professor of English at the University of Chicago, "This decay of belief in standards has infected the highest echelons of our social and political life." It has also infected important sectors of the church. Studies made at leading schools of religion reveal that belief in unchanging moral laws has largely given way to the view that "all guidelines are irrelevant"—that is, a fixed moral code must go. In other words, "decisions must come from man's sense of what the moment demands." That is called "situation ethics," meaning that instead of applying eternal moral principles to a situation, we let each situation determine the principle.

In my own denomination (Presbyterian) recently, a special committee was charged with writing a "brief contemporary statement of faith." The committee's draft of a proposed "Confession of 1967" replaced the ancient Westminster Confession's strong assertion of the Bible's "infallible truth and divine authority" with a description of the Bible as a "witness" to Christ as the incarnate Word—and a fallible one at that, since its "thought forms reflect views which were then current" and therefore require "literary and historical scholarship" as well as future "scientific developments" to separate the true from the false. This attempt to demote the Bible from final authority to a fallible witness has stirred a storm of protest in church circles.

That such uncertain theology has penetrated many leading schools of divinity, minimizing Bible teaching and leaving the Scriptures' importance in doubt, is obvious. Says Dr. Roger L. Shinn, Dean of Instruction at Union Theological Seminary, "In the 25 years that I've been studying theology, I've never seen the situation so chaotic." Naturally. When foundations are shaken, chaos ensues.

With seminary emphasis what it is today, it is not surprising that Biblical preaching in many churches has declined. Like most laymen, I go to church to hear heralded the mind of Christ, not the mind of man. I want to hear expounded the timeless truth contained in the Scriptures, the kind of preaching that gets its power from "Thus saith the Lord." Such preaching is hard to find these days. This may well explain the curious fact, revealed by latest church statistics as well as a Gallup poll, that while church membership is showing a steady rise, church attendance is steadily dropping.

To Fill the Vacuum

Another thing I've noted during long years on denominational and interdenominational boards and commissions is this: Whenever any official church body relegates the Bible and its teachings to a lesser place in its program, it almost always turns to activity in non-church fields to fill the vacuum. Thus we see church leadership everywhere expending vast time and energy to push the church into fields far outside its God-ordained jurisdiction.

Evangelism, traditionally interpreted as the means used to bring men and women to Christ and the church, has been given a completely new definition. Says Dr. Jitsuo Morikawa, secretary of evangelism of the American Baptist Convention, "Contemporary evangelism is moving away from winning souls one by one, to the evangelism of the structures of society." Says Dr. D. T. Niles, one of the World Council of Churches' leading figures, "The heart of Christianity is not concern for the soul but concern for the world."

Expressing this "concern," the church's new-type evangelists, without any notable competence in either statecraft or economics, are leaping headlong into such fundamentally secular concerns as federal aid to education, civil rights, urban renewal, the nation's foreign policy, and plugging for such controversial issues as the admission of Red China to the United Nations, disarmament, higher minimum wages, forcible union membership, etc.

As *Newsweek* recently noted, clergymen last year "defied police barriers to march in Selma, Ala., paraded before the Pentagon to protest the Vietnam war, condemned prayers in public schools, rallied Mexican and Filipino laborers in their strike against California fruit growers." From high church commissions and councils come regularly such sweeping statements as "A church that denies responsibility in economic affairs can offer no acceptable worship to God."

Crusading churchmen move easily from social and economic action into party politics. During the last Presidential campaign, an editorial appearing in *Christianity and Crisis* proclaimed: "Goldwater has set himself against the overwhelming consensus of Christian social doctrines enunciated by the churches. Christians when they vote should know that."

Through the Proper Instruments

I am not alone in disapproving of the trend. Publisher Clifford P. Morehouse, lay president of the Protestant Episcopal Church's house of deputies, recently counseled all makers of church polity and program to "guard constantly against the great danger of confusing their personal predilections with the will of the Almighty."

Similar counsel, largely unheeded, has come from other highly respected churchmen. Says Dr. David H. C. Read, minister of New York's Madison Avenue Presbyterian Church, "I find there is something incomplete, lopsided, sometimes even false about the new activism in the churches. Renewal of the church does not come from new forms of social action, however necessary these may be. It begins within. A church that sets out to do the works of God, spreading into every area of life, yet neglecting the living center of belief, is doomed not to renewal but to decay."

No one would seriously deny that the individual Christian must relate his conscience to the problems of the secular society of which he is a part. It is plainly his duty as a citizen to express his Christian convictions in economic, social and political affairs. Likewise, no one would deny the pulpit's right to speak out on civil issues where moral and spiritual principles are clearly involved.

However, action to correct existing ills in the secular society should be taken through secular organizations: political parties, chambers of commerce, labor unions, parent-teacher associations, service clubs and many others which can supply skilled leadership and techniques to do the job. To commit the church as a corporate body to controversial positions on which its members differ sharply is to divide the church into warring camps, stirring dissensions in the one place where spiritual unity should prevail.

When any individual church or church council, largely dominated by clergymen, issues statements on complex economic and political matters, giving the public the impression that it is speaking for the whole membership, the result is justifiable indignation on the part of the laity. "When I joined the church," writes one laymen from Park Ridge, Ill., "I stated my faith in Jesus Christ as my personal Saviour. I was not asked to subscribe to any special political, economic or social view. Is that now about to be changed?"

I find it difficult to understand that such protests do not seem to bother the church's self-styled "God's avant garde." "We will get real schisms over the church-in-the-world issue," admits the Rev. Donald Benedict of Chicago. "Some congregations are going to be split right up the middle in the next ten years."

Also less than pleased these days by the church's overwhelming preoccupation with civil affairs are America's lawmakers and civil authorities. I have a file full of letters from members of Congress expressing resentment over church pressures. Says one: "Separation between church and state is a principle deeply embedded in our tradition. Yet church leaders who would raise the loudest outcry if government attempted to interfere in any way with church matters see nothing contradictory in maintaining Washington lobbies and trying to dictate to Congress the kind of legislation which should be enacted on almost every conceivable economic, social and political subject."

From another distinguished Senator comes this: "I have been particularly distressed by the actions of many of our clergy and other church leaders who justify their violation of federal, state and local laws on the grounds that these are 'bad' laws and that the only way to correct them is to break them. Once it has been stated that any law need not be obeyed unless it is a 'good law,' the beginning of an end to rule by law has been initiated."

Highest Priority

By what Scriptural authority does the modern Christian church make this turnabout from its ancient mission? Christ himself made a clear distinction between the concerns of temporal and spiritual natures. He refused to enmesh himself or his followers in the economic, social and political problems of his day— problems certainly as serious as those we face today. When the Pharisees sought to entangle him in politics, asking him whether they should pay taxes to Rome, Jesus gave the classic answer: "Render unto Caesar the things that are Caesar's, and unto God the things that are God's."

At no time did he countenance civil disobedience or promote political pressure either to correct social evils or to advance his spiritual mission. His highest priority was given to measures for changing the hearts of men and women, knowing full well that changed men and women would in time change society—as indeed they have done all down the ages. He made it crystal-clear that we are to seek "first the kingdom of God and His righteousness"—carefully pointing out that "the kingdom is within you."

The church, during periods of its greatest influence, has always followed that lead. Only when, as during the Middle Ages, it forsook its spiritual mission to gain temporal power, has its real power languished. Succeeding church fathers, having learned from the Middle Ages, brought the church back to its rightful realm and insisted that it stay there. John Calvin, father of the Reformed tradition, was one among many who stated flatly that "the church has no Scriptural authority to speak outside the ecclesiastical field," warning that "meddling in politics" was divisive and inimical to the church's success.

If the church's "social activists" are to be halted from plunging the church again into areas where it has no jurisdiction, its concerned laymen and clergymen will have to make their voices heard more clearly in the high councils of their denominations.

To me, the church is the hope—perhaps the only hope—of the world. If it proclaims the Bread of Life, as it did in the past, it will so affect society that many of our prevalent social ills will disappear. But, as a visiting Church of England theologian remarked after extensive observation of U.S. churchmen's frenetic devotion to "social action," "It would be tragically ironic if the church, grown skeptical about God's power to redeem society by transforming human nature, were to fall into the same ideological error as communism and attempt to transform men by altering his environment."

Three

CARL HENRY WAS RIGHT*

Richard J. Mouw

I have an account to settle with Carl Henry. It is too late to personally settle it with him—although I hope the Lord eventually gives me the chance to do that in the hereafter. For now, though, I can at least set the record straight in the pages of this magazine, which Dr. Henry served so capably as *Christianity Today*'s first editor.

The story starts in the fall of 1967 when, as a Ph.D. student in philosophy at the University of Chicago, I received a phone call from Henry. A few weeks before I had sent an essay to him, outlining what I took to be a proper evangelical approach to the sub-discipline of social ethics. Henry told me that he very much liked my piece for its critique of liberal Protestantism's approach to the field, and wanted to publish it. He had only one revision to suggest—a minor one, he insisted. At the point where I said that it was indeed important for *the church* to on occasion take a stand on some specific question of social justice, he preferred

* This is an edited version of an essay used with permission here that originally appeared as Richard J. Mouw, "Carl Henry Was Right," *Christianity Today*, January 27, 2010, 30, http://www.christianitytoday.com/ct/2010/january/25.30.html.

to have me speak of the need for *individual Christians* to take such a stand.

The essay was the first piece I had ever submitted to any periodical beyond the world of on-campus publications. Needless to say, I was thrilled to get this kind of personal attention from one of my evangelical heroes. But I was also troubled by the change he was proposing. This was a period in my life when I had often felt alienated from evangelicalism because of what I saw as its failure to properly address issues raised by the civil rights struggle and the war in Southeast Asia. As a corrective, I wanted the church, *as church*, to acknowledge its obligation to speak to such matters. So I responded by telling Henry that I did not see his proposed change as a minor bit of editing. As much as I would be honored to see my essay appear as an article in *Christianity Today*, I said, I could not approve the formulation he was suggesting.

Henry thanked me for my time, and the conversation ended. But over the next two weeks he called several times, on each occasion urging me to accept some revision. At one point, for example, he asked me to approve a statement to the effect that the church should regularly articulate general principles that bear on social concerns, leaving it up to individuals to actively apply those principles to social specifics. I rejected that way of putting the case.

His final call set forth what he presented as some compromises. And I accepted them, albeit with some reluctance. Thus, where I had referred to "the church's duty" to address the topic of civil rights, he had substituted a revision that spoke, with some ambiguity, of a "Christian duty with respect to the civil rights of human beings."

And while he kept my insistence that the church itself must on occasion address social specifics, he limited its role to the making of negative pronouncements. He had me saying that the church can say "no" to things that are happening in the economic and political realms, without mentioning anything about the church legitimately endorsing specific remedial policies or practices.

Here is how the case was put in the published version of my essay: "It is often necessary for the church to take an unequivocal stand against prevailing economic, social, and political conditions, even where it is practically impossible to offer any solution" in terms that don't draw on extra-theological "'theoretical and empirical' analysis."[1]

Five Principles of Engagement

In his biography, *Confessions of a Theologian*, Henry makes it clear that there was much going on in the background during the time we were having those phone conversations. He goes into much detail about how, during this period, he was attempting to take on social issues in a reasonable manner in his editorial role, while also pleasing J. Howard Pew, president of the Sun Oil Company, who was contributing much-needed funding for the magazine.

Henry's obvious worries that Pew might be troubled by my article were confirmed by the fact that, after my essay appeared in print, Pew wrote to complain about what he saw as my insistence that "the church must often take a stand on economic, social, and political issues."[2] In reporting on this in his memoir, Henry explains how he defended me to Pew.

"Mouw's essay, I wrote in reply, had clearly stated that the church cannot offer legislative or military specifics, and is on safer ground, moreover, when it voices a negative verdict on the status quo."[3] Henry goes on to set forth what he explained to Pew as the five principles that had consistently guided his editorial policy on such matters in the magazine's pages:

1. The Bible is critically relevant to the whole of modern life and culture—the social-political arena included.

2. The institutional church has no mandate, jurisdiction, or competence to endorse political legislation

---

1. Richard J. Mouw, "The Task of 'Christian Social Ethics,'" *Christianity Today*, January 5, 1968, 5.

2. Carl F. H. Henry, *Confessions of a Theologian: An Autobiography* (Waco: Word, 1968), 270.

3. Henry, *Confessions of a Theologian*, 270.

or military tactics or economic specifics in the name of Christ.

3. The institutional church is divinely obliged to proclaim God's entire revelation, including the standards or commandments by which men and nations are to be finally judged, and by which they ought now to live and maintain social stability.

4. The political achievement of a better society is the task of all citizens, and individual Christians ought to be politically engaged to the limit of their competence and opportunity.

5. The Bible limits the proper activity of both government and church for divinely stipulated objectives—the former, for the preservation of justice and order, and the latter, for the moral-spiritual task of evangelizing the earth.

Having made his case to Pew, Henry reports that "thereafter I received only infrequent correspondence; little if any of that pertained to the church in politics."[4] By itself, of course, this could have been a sign that the oilman was satisfied with Henry's account. But the larger narrative does not allow for this interpretation of Pew's lack of communication. It is clear, for example, that Pew was instrumental in eventually moving Henry out of his editorship, desiring—as Henry puts it in his autobiography—"a more aggressive denunciation of ecumenical perspectives," particularly as they related to political and economic questions.[5]

Sometimes the Church Must Say No!

Here is what I need to say now about my youthful negotiations with Carl Henry: Henry was right and I was wrong. At the time I agreed to Henry's revision of my draft, I only grudgingly accepted

---

4. Henry, *Confessions of a Theologian*, 270–71.
5. Henry, *Confessions of a Theologian*, 290.

what I considered a less-than-fully satisfactory compromise arrangement. What I really wanted to say is that the church—in the form of both preaching and ecclesial pronouncements—could do more than merely utter a no to some social evils. There were times, I was convinced, that the church could rightly say a bold yes to specific policy-like solutions. I now see that youthful conviction as misguided. Henry was right, and I was wrong.

In pushing me on this subject, Henry was not merely trying to avoid offending a significant funding source. The second point of the five principles that Henry summarized for Pew had long been a major theme in his reflections on the church's public calling.

For example, in his now-classic 1947 jeremiad, *The Uneasy Conscience of Modern Fundamentalism*, Henry had complained that the evangelical ministers of his day were not addressing important social concerns. In the early pages of his book, he tells us that he had recently posed this question to a group of evangelical pastors about their preaching:

> How many of you, during the past six months, have preached a sermon devoted in large part to a condemnation of such social evils as aggressive warfare, racial hatred and intolerance, the liquor traffic, exploitation of labor or management, or the like—a sermon containing not merely an incidental or illustrative reference, but directed mainly against such evils and proposing the *framework* in which you think solution is possible?[6]

Not one of the pastors, he reports, could testify that he had preached such a sermon.

Note that in urging pastors to address social concerns, Henry is careful to limit their role to the no-saying function. He wants from them a "condemnation" of selected social evils. They are to speak "against" such things. What they are to offer in positive terms is not practical solutions, but the "proposing [of a] *framework* in which you think solution is possible" (emphasis mine).

---

6. Carl F. H. Henry, *The Uneasy Conscience of Modern Fundamentalism* (1947; repr., Grand Rapids: Eerdmans, 2003), 4. Emphasis added. See page 17 in this volume.

In the months immediately preceding my telephone conversation with Henry, he had taken up this theme at some length in *Christianity Today*'s pages. In a feature article, along with an accompanying editorial in the September 15, 1967, issue, Henry praised Princeton University ethicist Paul Ramsey for the way he had criticized ecumenical Protestantism in his recent book, *Who Speaks for the Church?* In particular, Henry praised Ramsey's critique of ecumenical Protestantism's way of issuing what Henry describes (paraphrasing Ramsey) as "a staggering number of resolutions that support particular positions."[7] And the issue for Ramsey was not just the sheer number of pronouncements, but also a methodology that flowed from a defective theology. Henry quotes Ramsey's harsh verdict: "Identification of Christian social ethics with specific partisan proposals that clearly are not the only ones that may be characterized as Christian and as morally acceptable comes close to the original New Testament meaning of *heresy*."[8]

While endorsing the general thrust of Ramsey's case, Henry was careful not to let evangelicals off the hook. This important critique should be the occasion, Henry insisted, for evangelicals "to consider what they may properly say to the world about social justice." The church is obliged to "declare the criteria by which nations will ultimately be judged, and the divine standards to which man and society must conform if civilization is to endure." What the Bible actually says about such matters should "belong legitimately to pulpit proclamation." Evangelicals, he urged, needed to do a more effective job of "enunciating theological and moral principles that bear upon public life."[9]

This did not mean for Henry that the church should get into endorsing specific solutions. A constant theme in his writings was that the church as such has neither the competence nor the

7. Carl F. H. Henry, "A Challenge to Ecumenical Politicians," *Christianity Today*, September 15, 1967, 3.

8. Paul Ramsey, *Who Speaks for the Church? A Critique of the 1966 Geneva Conference on Church and Society* (Nashville: Abingdon, 1967), 56.

9. Editorial, "An Ecumenical Bombshell," *Christianity Today*, September 15, 1967, 28.

authority to address political or economic specifics. He would usually add, though—probably with the memory of Nazi Germany in mind—that there may be "emergency situations" in which the church would have clear mandate from God to address specific evils. But in the normal course of things, the church should leave it up to individuals to take a very general mandate to think and act Christianly in the public arena.

What Christians Can Do Together

So, again, Henry was right about all of that. If I still have a slight misgiving about the way he made his case, it has to do with an impression Henry gives about what takes place *after* the church provides the Christian community with biblically grounded general principles. He suggests that once believers have heard what the church has to say, it's up to them to struggle individually with moving toward specifics.

Another of my theological heroes, Abraham Kuyper, would have agreed completely with Henry about the limits of what the church, as a worshiping and catechizing community, can do by way of addressing issues of public life. But Kuyper would have insisted that, between the gathered church and individual Christians going out into the world to struggle with applications to specifics, there is an important intermediate area of activity. Christians must form a variety of organizations that focus on specific areas of cultural involvement, in order to engage in the kind of communal reflection necessary to develop a Christian mind for the area in question.

This means that it is important, say, for Christians who are deeply involved in policies and practices relating to concern for the poor to develop specific proposals building on the general principles proclaimed by that church, by deliberating on these matters in groups that have the expertise to struggle with them. And it is even appropriate to present those policy proposals as Christian-inspired specifics, even if they move well beyond what the church—as church—has a right to say.

In our own day, it may be especially important for the church to see to it that this "beyond the worshiping church" communal discussion actually takes place. A good model is the creative outreach embodied in the very creative Center for Faith and Work, sponsored by New York's Redeemer Presbyterian Church, where laypeople can meet to think more specifically about how to serve the Lord beyond the worshiping community's borders.

But that is not so much a disagreement with Henry as it is a further development of his important views about church and the public arena. I am not alone in owing a debt of gratitude to Henry for his pioneering—and courageous—efforts to encourage a more mature evangelical discipleship in the broad reaches of culture. I hope others will join me in continuing to learn from him how best to search out remedies for an evangelicalism that still suffers from an "uneasy conscience."

PART 2

PRINCIPLES OF RESPONSIBILITY

Four

A PEARL AND A LEAVEN

The Twofold Call of the Gospel

Jessica Driesenga

G od has given humanity two great tasks. First, "fill the earth and subdue it" (Gen. 1:28)—a call to societal life; to create art, participate in politics and social action, engage in economics, and in all sorts of facets of our society; and to take the world that has been given to us and create something with it. Second, "go and make disciples of all nations" (Matt. 28:19)—an evangelistic call to preach the gospel, a precious task for the people of God to tell others of the saving work of Christ. What, then, is the relationship between these two tasks? While a cursory look at how Christians engage these two tasks may suggest that we must choose one to the detriment of the other, the Dutch theologian Herman Bavinck (1854–1921) points us to an understanding of the complementarity of God's twofold call to engage in societal life and make disciples.

These two great tasks can often seem as though they oppose each other. Either the Christian understands the good news of Jesus Christ as propelling us into the public square and as solely focused on culture making or correcting the social ills of the day through social action *or* the Christian understands the good news of Jesus Christ as a treasured thing that must be sought out, then proclaimed to all the world, but kept at a distance from anything that might soil it or dilute its power. The gospel can either be fully engaged in society or held at some distance from all cultural activities. The message that there is a dichotomy between these two tasks is pervasive. One pastor, reflecting on his time serving a church, realized that "in sermon after sermon I had called [my congregation] to give more time, more money, more energy to the work of the church. Little did I understand or affirm their callings in the world. I had inadvertently created a secular/sacred divide in which the 'sacred' calling of the church was pitted against their 'secular' callings in the world."[1]

When we survey Christians' posture toward the world, it can seem as though there is an either-or decision to be made: either choose to be a part of the world or separate yourself from it for the sake of the gospel.

If this either-or is indeed correct, we find ourselves in a bit of a quandary trying to make sense of someone like Martin Luther King Jr., a church leader who also was involved in significant social reforms. Perhaps someone like him should be enough to dissuade us from having to choose between these two great tasks God has given humanity. Put more strongly, perhaps King helps to expose the artificial separation that is sometimes created between the cultural mandate ("fill the earth and subdue it") and the Great Commission ("go and make disciples of all nations"). Deeming this an artificial separation, of course, implies that these tasks ought to be seen as necessary counterparts to each other. Rather than an either-or, the call to make disciples and engage in societal life is a *both-and*. These two tasks are complementary.

The complementarity of these two tasks is wonderfully illustrated by Herman Bavinck, who understands the gospel to be both a *pearl* and a *leaven*. These two metaphors, mixed as they may seem, are Bavinck's way of understanding the dual tasks given to humanity: to preserve and preach the good news of Christ and to take the world that has been given to us and make something of it. Rather than understanding these two

---

1. Skye Jethani, "Uncommon Callings," *Leadership Journal*, Winter 2013, http://www.christianitytoday.com/le/2013/winter/uncommon-callings.html.

tasks as distinct and perhaps even antithetical, his joining of the metaphors of pearl and leaven helps us to understand how these two tasks function together.

Bavinck's metaphors come from two of the shortest parables in the Gospel of Matthew, where Jesus describes the kingdom of heaven as a pearl of great value and as a leaven. First, Jesus teaches, "The kingdom of heaven is like leaven that a woman took and hid in three measures of flour, till it was all leavened" (Matt. 13:33). Jesus later says, "The kingdom of heaven is like a merchant in search of fine pearls, who, on finding one pearl of great value, went and sold all that he had and bought it" (Matt. 13:45–46). Bavinck uses these images to describe what the gospel proclaims and how that proclamation is manifested in society. In his discussions of the gospel as pearl and the gospel as leaven, he points to the reality that the gospel must be seen as *both* a pearl and a leaven.

To understand Bavinck, we must note the priority that he places on the gospel as a pearl, that is, the heavenly, spiritual reality of the kingdom of God and the righteousness of Christ. He writes,

> Even if Christianity had resulted in nothing more than this spiritual and holy community, even if it had not brought about any modification in earthly relationships ... it would still be and remain something of everlasting worth. The significance of the gospel does not depend on its influence on culture, its usefulness for life today; it is a *treasure* in itself, a *pearl* of great value, even if it might not be a leaven.[2]

The spiritual reality of the kingdom of God and the truth of the gospel is of infinite value to us. It is a pearl, something worth seeking after at any cost. The value of this spiritual reality should not be downplayed in the slightest, regardless of whether it has any tangible benefit to our world today. What Christ inaugurated on earth, the kingdom of heaven, must be understood as

---

2. Herman Bavinck, "Christian Principles and Social Relationships," in *Essays on Religion, Science, and Society*, ed. John Bolt, trans. Harry Boonstra and Gerrit Sheeres (Grand Rapids: Baker Academic, 2008), 141. Emphasis added.

a heavenly treasure; God's gift of righteousness, salvation, and eternal life, obtained by faith, has unspeakable value. It is the pearl of great price.

If that were all Bavinck had to say, though, he may be at fault for creating an either-or situation between either the treasure found *within* the church or the church going out *into* the world. Though Bavinck places priority on the gospel understood as a pearl, that is not the end of the matter. Instead, in another work, he considers the reforming power of the gospel:

> The truth and value of Christianity certainly does not depend on the fruits which it has borne for civilization and culture: it has its own independent value; it is the realization of the kingdom of God on earth; and it does not make its truth depend, after a utilitarian or pragmatical fashion, on what men here have accomplished with the talents entrusted to them.... But, nevertheless, the kingdom of heaven, while a pearl of great price, is also a leaven which permeates the whole of the meal; godliness is profitable unto all things having the promise of the life which now is, and that which is to come.[3]

The people of God are given a promise of eternal life in the future, but are also given promises for life in our world today. Godliness, that is, keeping the commandments of God, does not only have eternal rewards. It bears fruit in society, exerting the influence of the gospel as a leavening agent throughout the world. The gospel has a tangible and important impact in our world today, bearing great fruit in society. The gospel, as a leaven, has culture-making, culture-swaying, and culture-transforming power.

This leavening, the influencing power of the gospel throughout the world, does not operate on its own. It comes from the core of the gospel, the pearl of great price. As Bavinck notes, "so from this center it influences all earthly relationships in a reforming

---

3. Herman Bavinck, *The Philosophy of Revelation* (1908; repr., Grand Rapids: Baker, 1979), 268–69.

and renewing way."[4] The leavening power of the gospel does not exist without the regeneration, faith, and conversion of humanity, the heavenly treasure, or pearl, gifted to humanity in Christ. But, in the restoring of one's relationship with God through the work of Christ, the gospel can go on to have a leavening effect in the world. The pearl has priority over the leaven, but this does not lead Bavinck away from stressing the importance of the gospel as both pearl and leaven. The gospel both creates a new community, restoring the relationship between God and his people, *and* has a robust influence on the present society.

The gospel is a transcendent pearl of great price and a transforming leavening agent in the world. Indeed, according to Bavinck, the gospel can only transform what it first has transcended. First, people come to know the spiritual matters of the kingdom of God. On its own, without any influence on society, this is a pearl of the greatest value. However, once discovered, the gospel is also a leaven, providing the impetus for the Christian's involvement in society. The gospel does not just remain set apart, kept as a precious treasure apart from the world and transcending the world. It is also acts in the world as a leaven that permeates the whole, transforming the world.

The artificial separation between making disciples and engagement in the world, or between the pure preaching of the gospel and social action, must be dispelled. Both are important and ought to be seen as complementary and reciprocal. The gospel is both a pearl and a leaven! But, we still need a way of understanding the distinction between the two tasks and sorting out *who* is responsible for each task.

Bavinck's images of pearl and leaven helpfully correspond with two other images that Bavinck and others in the neo-Calvinist tradition use to distinguish between two senses of the church: the church as institute and the church as organism. This distinction between these two conceptions of the church is critical to understanding the role of the church in the twofold task given to humanity by God, and this distinction is the key to understanding

---

4. Bavinck, "Christian Principles and Social Relationships," 142.

where the responsibility lies for the tasks of gospel preaching and social action.[5]

On the one hand, the church is understood as an institution. The church as an institution is gathered around the Word and sacraments; it corresponds to how the church is often identified, that is, by its corporate worship, the offices of the church, the official programs of the church, and administration of the Word and sacrament. The church as an institution guards, protects, and proclaims the pearl of great price. On the other hand, the church is understood as an organism. The church as an organism consists of the communal life of believers; it corresponds to the many vocations of the people of God—not limited to a formal or liturgical setting—as they spread out in the world. The church as an organism acts as a leavening agent in the world through the callings of individual Christians. The tasks of the church as organism and as institute are distinct, but both are important.

God has called humanity to fill the earth and subdue it and to go and make disciples of all nations. Often these are seen as opposing tasks, pressuring us to choose either the church or the world. We must either make disciples, preach a pure gospel, and remain separate from the world *or* engage in culture and society, working to transform and renew culture through the power of the Spirit. The opposition of these tasks often leads to emphasizing one, to the detriment of the other. However, this ought not be the case. Bavinck helpfully articulates the necessity of both of these tasks. The gospel is both pearl *and* leaven. The church is both institute *and* organism. Bavinck's use of corresponding metaphors and distinctions—pearl and leaven, institute and organism—disallows the dichotomy without collapsing the categories. There are indeed multiple tasks of the church, tasks which are rightly understood to be given to different manifestations of the church. The tasks of the church as institute—preaching, sacraments, and discipline—are not the

---

5. Herman Bavinck, *Reformed Dogmatics*, vol. 4, *Holy Spirit, Church, and New Creation*, ed. John Bolt, trans. John Vriend (Grand Rapids: Baker Academic, 2008), 329–30.

tasks of the church as organism, which goes out into society and engages in culture making and social action. But for Bavinck, differentiation does not lead to a negation of one or the other. The gospel is both a pearl of great price and a leavening agent throughout all the world.

Five

A NEO-CALVINIST ECCLESIOLOGY*

David T. Koyzis

Decades ago, a young couple of my acquaintance who had been attracted to the neo-calvinist vision of the comprehensive lordship of Jesus Christ over the whole of life, confessed to me that they were no longer attending church. If all of life is encompassed in principle by the kingdom of God, they reasoned, what is the point of affiliating with a particular institution labeled "the Church"? They were not alone. I knew of others who took a similar position.

They were unaware that neo-Calvinism boasts a robust ecclesiology, one in which the church institution has a central, though not all-encompassing, place.

To understand this we must begin by distinguishing two meanings of the word *church*, which we cannot afford to confuse if we are to properly discern the norms God has given for human society. Abraham Kuyper distinguishes between *church as organism* and *church as institution*, which is a development of previous

* This is an edited version of an essay used with permission here that originally appeared as David T. Koyzis, "A Neocalvinist Ecclesiology," *Comment*, September 1, 2011, https://www.cardus.ca/comment/article/4566/a-neocalvinist-ecclesiology/.

distinctions including Calvin's distinction between invisible and visible church. (While Calvin's distinction relates to the differences between divine and human perception of membership in each, Kuyper's addresses the range of activities encompassed by each.)

The church as organism is basically the *corpus Christi*—the *body of Christ*. Those who are in Christ are members of his body, with its diversity of gifts contributing to its unity of faith in its Lord and Savior (Rom. 12:4–8; 1 Cor. 12). As Christians, our membership in this body is not limited to what we do on Sunday in the formal liturgical setting. Rather, it takes in our whole lives in all of our activities (1 Cor. 10:31; Col. 3:17). We live out our marriages, families, employment, and political lives as members of Christ's church. In this sense the church is all-embracing, not simply one community among many.

The church as institution, by contrast, is a *differentiated community with its own specific task, internal organization and office-bearers*. Thus understood, the church is not the same as the state, the family, the school, or any other community found in a mature, differentiated society. Accordingly church office-bearers should not attempt to dictate to political leaders, business executives, and university administrators, all of whom have a divinely mandated responsibility for stewardship over their own particular spheres. The notion that, say, bishops or church elders should appoint prime ministers or preside over labor unions is a nonstarter for the simple reason that the former would thereby exceed the proper limits of their own offices.

The institutional church has a central role to play in the lives of believers for which there can be no substitute. Indeed Calvin devotes most of the fourth volume of his *Institutes of the Christian Religion* to the "Holy Catholic Church" and its ordinary means of grace. For Calvin, the church is found wherever the true ministry of Word and sacraments is present. This ministry is conducted by office-holders ordained for the purpose. So central is this institution to the life of faith that Calvin argues that moral flaws, and even minor doctrinal differences, in the visible church can never constitute sufficient reason for separating ourselves from its communion. Calvin calls those wilfully withdrawing from the church traitors and apostates.

Although I spent my first years in a church with a strong institutional ecclesiology based on the Westminster Standards, it was not until I read Dutch philosopher Herman Dooyeweerd (1894–1977) that I gained a renewed appreciation for the place of the institutional church. In the third volume of his *New Critique of Theoretical Thought*, Dooyeweerd makes an important distinction between institutional communities and voluntary associations. Institutional communities are those that embrace their members in an intensive way, often for life, and apart from their individual wills. One is born to membership in a particular family; one does not choose one's parents or siblings. Similarly, one is a citizen of a particular state by birth, although one might, of course, assume another citizenship later in life. In our society we enter marriage voluntarily, but once we have done so, we are said to have entered the estate or *institution* of matrimony, which makes claims on our lives and affections that we cannot simply bring to an end at will.

What about the church? According to Dooyeweerd, the gathered congregation is indeed an institution and cannot be recast as a mere voluntary association. A voluntary association is one whose members freely enter and quit at their pleasure. Their obligations toward the association last for only as long as they are willing to accept them. I may be a member of a bird-watching society for a time. I have joined at some point in the past, paid my dues, accepted its bylaws, attended its meetings and participated in its activities, especially its jaunts into the forest to observe a colorful panoply of feathered species. At some point, however, I tire of bird-watching, preferring chess instead. When I quit the bird-watching society, there are no hard feelings. I have in no way endangered the group or myself. No one begrudges me the right to leave and go elsewhere. Similarly, if I leave my place of employment and take a job elsewhere, no one would deny me the right to do so. People do this everyday, with no harm to the larger society.

It is not so with the church. Under the predominant influence of liberalism in our society, we are often inclined to reduce the array of communal formations to mere voluntary associations. Accordingly we tend to view the local church congregation similarly: as a mere association of converted individuals. This attitude is bolstered by an advertisement frequently appearing on the church pages of newspapers and phone books: "Attend the church of your choice." We are implicitly invited to look at the church listings as a kind of ecclesiastical smorgasbord in which we are free to "shop" for a church home that best fits our own priorities, proclivities, and lifestyles. The churches tend to position themselves in such a way as to appeal to a specific "market share," scheduling, say, traditional and contemporary liturgies to try to bring in specific demographics. A thriving church is one which has picked up a large share of the ecclesiastical "market" and has thus successfully positioned itself as a powerful player in what is now seen as a kind of competitive game. Numbers are everything, as these enable large budgets, big buildings, and flourishing programs.

By contrast, Dooyeweerd argues that the gathered church is an institution which we cannot simply quit at will without doing potentially irreparable spiritual damage to ourselves and to the other communities of which we are part. Such a church is "an institutionally organized community of Christian believers in the administration of the Word and the sacraments."[1] It is called into being by the divine covenant and is built on the historical power of the incarnate Word. The gathered church is above all a *confessional* church and not a *national* church. A church that undertakes to unite all members of a nation can only be a deformation of the church type. Similarly, efforts at ecumenical cooperation that ignore basic differences in confession risk suppressing the very nature of the church institution. Any claimed unity that comes of these efforts will inevitably be illusory. The

---

1. Herman Dooyeweerd, *A New Critique of Theoretical Thought*, vol. 3, trans. David H. Freeman and H. de Jongste (Phillipsburg: Presbyterian & Reformed, 1969), 539.

church's confession is precisely in the incarnate Word, Jesus Christ. Apart from this there can be no church.

Following Calvin, Dooyeweerd affirms that the church institution has its own organization and offices, which are fundamentally different from those of other organizations, including the state. The internal organization of the church is not an indifferent matter but is grounded in God's word revelation, namely, Scripture. While Luther is content to leave this matter in the hands of the civil magistrate, Calvin and Dooyeweerd are not: "All the communicant members have been invested with the general office (διακονία) to cooperate in the work of formation and reformation of the Church-institution, in the election of the special office-bearers, etc."[2] The specific offices are not simply up to the discretion of individual congregations or church members along ostensibly democratic lines; they must accord with the structural principle of the institutional church itself as a community of faith rooted in Scripture.

This raises the difficult and historically divisive issue of baptism, which Dooyeweerd touches on in his discussion of the church. According to Dooyeweerd, the church's institutional character is intimately bound up with the baptism of its youngest members: "The institutional community of the Church receives the children of Christian parents as its members by baptism and as such they continue to belong to this community through a bond independent of their will, until they reach their years of discretion."[3] This stands in marked contrast to those church communities "based on the personal qualities of converted individuals."[4] Because the church is not a mere association, it can never be anchored in the shifting whims of individual persons, however good and holy they might be. It can only be anchored in the divine covenant of grace and in the rock of our salvation, Jesus Christ. With Calvin once again, Dooyeweerd accepts that children of believers are heirs of the covenant and thus members of the visible church. As such, parents are mandated to raise their children in the faith.

---

2. Dooyeweerd, *New Critique of Theoretical Thought*, 538.

3. Dooyeweerd, *New Critique of Theoretical Thought*, 187.

4. Dooyeweerd, *New Critique of Theoretical Thought*, 532.

Dooyeweerd makes two more affirmations to complete his ecclesiology. First, the institutional church is fully present in the gathered congregation, something we have already hinted at above. The reformers recognized "that the *local congregation* is the *primary* institutional manifestation of the Church of Jesus Christ."[5] This Dooyeweerd affirms against those who would find the starting point of the church at the pinnacle of an ecclesiastical hierarchy distinct from and presiding over the congregations. In this he believes he follows apostolic usage, which speaks of the local church in the singular and several local churches in the plural, "but never of a Church in the sense of the fusion of all local congregations into a more comprehensive organization."[6] It is by no means incidental that Dooyeweerd's own denomination, the Reformed Churches in the Netherlands, had a plural name and refrained from assuming the singular label of *church*.

Second, while the institutional church is central in that it carries the life-giving Word and sacraments to the believer, it does not possess innate superiority over other societal communities and relationships. All of these have their worth and find their meaning only in their radical dependence on the creating and redeeming God, and not in their relationship to the institutional church. This is a key implication of Kuyper's notion of sphere sovereignty: there is no human community that presides in an absolute sense over all others. The institutional church has its own mandate, as do state, marriage, family, and the plethora of voluntary associations making up the fabric of an ordinary human society. These communities are dependent in a direct and ultimate sense on the grace of God rather than on some other supposed overarching and all-embracing human community.

How might Dooyeweerd's ecclesiology change the way we approach the gathered local church? To begin with, we are not simply taking out membership in an ethnic or social club. We are not joining an association of like-minded people for our own chosen ends. We are in fact submitting ourselves to an institution which Calvin, following the early church fathers, goes so far as

---

5. Dooyeweerd, *New Critique of Theoretical Thought*, 559.
6. Dooyeweerd, *New Critique of Theoretical Thought*, 559.

to call our mother. From the outset of our life in Christ we are subject to her authority and discipline as well as receiving from her bosom the Word and sacraments that nourish us to eternal life in the coming new heaven and new earth. We dare not neglect the institutional church and the means of grace which offer such nourishment.

Six

ABRAHAM KUYPER, THE INSTITUTIONAL CHURCH, AND SOCIO-POLITICAL ENGAGEMENT

Michael R. Wagenman

E vangelical churches have a rich history of equipping Christians to bear witness to the gospel of Jesus Christ. Names like Billy Graham, Francis Schaeffer, and C. S. Lewis ignite our memories and spark our imaginations of what it means to be an evangelical Christian. Even more contemporary figures like Shane Claiborne, Russell Moore, and Tim Keller have been used by God to reach a new generation with the gospel.

At times, though, evangelical churches have struggled to know how the church as an institution should relate to the other institutions of society. Does the church have direct input on contemporary public issues through alignment with a particular political party? *Should* the church have such input? Or is the institutional church to keep out of the messy business of politics and social issues? The result has been periodic pendulum swings between withdrawal from the world and outright culture warfare.

One noteworthy theologian who sought to influence nearly every aspect of his culture with Christianity and who offered many thoughts on how Christians and churches could be most effective for the kingdom of God was Abraham Kuyper (1837– 1920). Not only as theologian and pastor but also as journalist, politician, and labor organizer, Kuyper can guide the evangelical church through the politically charged and polarized culture many Christians inhabit today. One important area where Kuyper is helpful is on how institutions—churches, governments, and so on—relate in society.

Society in God's Creation

Kuyper believed that God's creation contained great potential. Over time, the potential built into creation would manifest various distinct but interrelated arenas of societal activity. The three most basic arenas or spheres of society were the family, the state, and the church, and each had its own inner logic and direct accountability to Christ. Kuyper called this "sphere sovereignty," meaning that each sphere of society was unique under the sovereignty of God.

For example, the family is unique for the nurturing of children. The state is unique for the restraint of evil and the exercise of justice. The church is unique for the worship of God and the redemption of rebellious human beings. Thus, a family should not function as if it were the state. And the state should not function as if it were a business. And the church should not function as if it were a bowling league. In fact, it is when a particular sphere of creation begins to function in the way unique to *another* sphere that major problems develop. Just imagine if a government were to relate to its citizens the way a business relates to its employees!

The Church in Society

The important thing to note about Kuyper's understanding of God's creation of human society is that the church is one among many societal institutions. The church is not the central institution but neither is it sidelined off on the margins, disconnected from the rest of society. The church doesn't control society but it isn't gagged from making a contribution either. The church is one institution amid a diversity of other institutions in society.

But what is the unique role the church plays in society? It is the question behind a perennial complaint one hears whenever the church (or church agencies) speak publicly on social issues. Some have the view that the church ought to concern itself with the gospel and leave political or social involvement to lay Christians.

This is where Kuyper's insights on the church as an institution are so helpful. Kuyper made the distinction between the church as an institution and the church as an organism. The institutional church is the gathered church, under ordained leadership, for the official worship of God. The organic church is the scattered church, the life of every Christian outside the four walls of the church building during the course of the week. And Kuyper taught that it is the role of the organic church to have a direct involvement with the social and political issues of the day.

In contrast, Kuyper taught that the institutional church has an *indirect* relationship with social and political issues. Unfortunately, some have interpreted this reality to mean that the church has *no* relationship of consequence to social issues.[1] But this would be a misunderstanding of Kuyper saying the relationship is *indirect*. The reason for this is that Kuyper taught that the unique calling of the institutional church was the contextualized and comprehensive proclamation of the gospel. The gospel doesn't dictate a particular governmental policy but the gospel has some applicability to every issue of human life.

It is a central tenet of evangelical and Reformed Christianity that the church exists to proclaim the gospel. Kuyper's contribution to this is to remind the institutional church that it glorifies God by proclaiming the gospel, which is *for the world*. That is, Kuyper followed Paul's teaching in Colossians 1 that Christ created all things, all things have fallen into sin, but Christ is redeeming all things. This means that the gospel is comprehensive in scope. It has to do with everything. It is the task of the church, therefore, to contextualize this comprehensive gospel,

---

1. See, for instance, Edgar Young Mullins, *Christianity at the Cross Roads* (New York: George H. Doran Co., 1924). And compare also Carl F. H. Henry, *The Uneasy Conscience of Modern Fundamentalism* (1947; repr., Grand Rapids: Eerdmans, 2003).

which will mean proclaiming the gospel as it gives insight and Christian trajectory to social and political issues.

Clearly, this doesn't mean that the institutional church is a specialist in everything. The church doesn't know which governmental policy will solve grinding poverty but the church is called to proclaim the gospel's requirement of compassion and justice for the poor. The church isn't skilled in knowing precisely which policies will restrict environmental degradation but the church is called to proclaim the gospel's call to stewardship and self-control for God's new-creation people.

It should be clear, then, that calls for the church to stick to the gospel alone and allow others to address the social and political challenges is either a false dichotomy or a means to limiting the gospel's scope. Kuyper's thought, on the other hand, prevents a wedge from being driven between the church and the society in which it lives. The institutional church must proclaim the comprehensive gospel. Otherwise the church is only concerning itself with *part* of God's creation.

Reimagining Church and Gospel

Kuyper's thoughts on the church's relationship with society prevent the church from marginalizing itself through either introspection or withdrawal from the world. Rather, Kuyper helps the church reimagine itself and its task of engaging the whole world with the gospel. There are two important ways in which Kuyper challenges our understanding of church.

The first is that Kuyper forces us to think deeply about how the church can take its historical and cultural context seriously. The whole point of Kuyper's thought in this regard is that the institutional church is a dialogue partner in the marketplace of civic institutions on important social and political matters. Kuyper envisioned a church (even as an institution) that was deeply embedded in and responsible to its context with the gospel. How will society hear the nuances and details of the gospel's application unless the church proclaims it comprehensively? The people of God, the organic church, cannot have a direct role in social or political issues unless the institutional church shows the way of the gospel for them.

The second way Kuyper's understanding can challenge us today is by forcing us to reimagine the sheer comprehensiveness of the gospel. Evangelicals know—and Kuyper reminds us—that the institutional church is called to proclaim the gospel. But if we're honest, we know that we tend to focus only on those areas of the gospel that strike us as "religious" or "spiritual" in nature. But for the church to be responsible with the whole gospel to its historical and cultural context means that we need to reimagine the amazingly comprehensive gospel of Jesus Christ. The institutional church's preaching shouldn't be myopic, hermetically sealing the church off from the world. The church can't proclaim a gospel that has holes in it. Rather, the comprehensive proclamation of the gospel—in contextually applicable ways—equips the church to more faithfully and effectively play its role in God's creation. The institutional church's proclamation of the gospel should apply just as wide as God's redemptive interest—which, according to Paul in Colossians 1, is "all things."

Why Has the Church Become So Hesitant?

Why is it that calls for the church to proclaim the gospel's comprehensiveness, especially as the gospel relates to social and political issues, make us anxious and hesitant? Clearly, one answer is the ease with which gospel proclamation can be driven by ideology. Every preacher knows the tensions between what Scripture says and what we want Scripture to say. But I don't think this is reason enough to reduce the gospel's application. If the church's proclamation of the gospel fails to address the social and political issues people are thinking about, the institutional church fails to be the incarnational presence of Jesus in the world, never really moving "into the neighborhood" as Jesus did (John 1:14, *The Message*).

Another possible reason for the church's or Christians' hesitance with this call for comprehensive gospel proclamation is the errors and abuses of the church's shortsightedness in history. But I think a bigger part of the answer lies in the stories we've told ourselves in evangelical and Reformed churches for a long while now. The Christian philosopher Nicholas Wolterstorff has said, "Over and over the church, when confronted by social realities that are unjust but that it prefers not to change, retreats into spirituality."[2]

That is, as Christians today, part of the story we tell ourselves is that Christianity is about spirituality and morality rather than public or political life. Over against this dualistic way of thinking about the Christian faith, Kuyper follows Scripture and insists that the entire world is God's creation, the entire world has rebelled against God in sin, and the entire world is being redeemed by Christ. Instead of a dualistic gospel, a gospel with holes in it, the gospel of Jesus Christ is truly about what God is doing in the whole world—and, oftentimes, through us, his ambassadors.

We would also do well to remember that the institutional church's proclamation is made up of both what is said *and what is not said*. If the institutional church remains silent about all the important issues facing the human community and nonhuman world today, that silence would communicate something incorrect about the God revealed in Jesus Christ who is renewing "all things." The gospel proclaimed by the institutional church shapes us today and shapes the next generation tomorrow and thereby creates the realities we live in, the laws we enact, and the doctrines we formulate. How unfaithful it would be if the church only preached a portion of the gospel, God's people were only partly discipled, and the world was only partly renewed.

The result of this hesitancy to give the gospel—and its proclamation by the institutional church—its fullest articulation and application is that the church gags itself and perpetuates ideas about God and God's world that are not true. The church may not turn the gospel into fiction. It is a fiction that the gospel is only interested in things that are spiritual. If the gospel is to be comprehensively proclaimed, Kuyper would encourage us to resolve

---

2. Nicholas Wolterstorff, *Hearing the Call: Liturgy, Justice, Church, and World*, ed. Mark R. Gornik and Gregory Thompson (Grand Rapids: Eerdmans, 2011), 213.

our hesitancy and give voice to what God is doing in the world right down to the level of contemporary socio-political issues.

A Failed Ambassador?

I'm very thankful for the reminders Abraham Kuyper gives for the church and its ministry of proclaiming the gospel to the world. Through Kuyper's insights into the church's relationship to society, I'm reminded that the gospel is about the nitty-gritty of life in the world. I'm reminded that when the institutional church fails to properly contextualize the comprehensive gospel in the here and now, that's when the church fails to be the ambassador of Jesus Christ in the world. It is in instances like that when the church has allowed the norms and expectations of the fallen world to dictate and control the terms by which the church's life, ministry, and witness are practiced.

We know that there are important social and political issues in the world today. The institutional church, proclaiming the comprehensive gospel, is one of the dialogue partners in the marketplace of civic institutions.

PART 3

PRACTICES OF RESPONSIBILITY

Seven

THE CHURCH'S ROLE
IN SOCIAL JUSTICE*

Calvin P. Van Reken

L et me begin by calling attention to a distinction that is essential to thinking clearly about the issue of the church's
engagement of social issues: the distinction between the church
as an *institution* and the church as an *organism*. This distinction is between two ways of thinking of, or conceptualizing, the
church, and thus two ways of speaking about it. Neither one of
these ways is right and the other wrong, nor one proper and the
other improper—they both have their legitimate use.

One can think of the church as an institution, or the *mater
fidelium* as Berkhof calls it. The church as an institution is a
formal organization that sets out to accomplish a specific purpose.
It is an agent. It can do things; it can say things; it has its own
voice. As an institution, it has its own purposes and plans, its
own structure and officers, and its own mission. It has its own
proper sphere. In many ways it parallels other institutions, like
governments or schools. Working for the church makes you a

* This essay used with permission here originally appeared as Calvin
P. Van Reken, "The Church's Role in Social Justice," *Calvin Theological
Journal* 34 (1999): 198–202.

church worker, and the work you do is church work. (Note that not all work done by Christians is church work.)

One can also conceive of the church as an organism, or the *mater coetus* as Berkhof calls it. This is to consider the church as the body of believers, the communion of believers. *It differs from the institutional church in that it refers to the church, not as a unified organization, but rather as an aggregate of individual believers.* In this aggregate, each Christian is, of course, a personal agent. Each Christian has a purpose and a call in God's plan. Each has a vocation, a calling, whether it is as a plumber, a teacher, or a politician.

From this also follows a distinction between *church work*, which is the work that a Christian does as an agent of the institutional church, and *kingdom work*, which is the work that a Christian does in service of his Lord—but not as an agent of the institutional church.

The Christian's Involvement in Society

The question for this article is *not* whether individual Christians or groups of Christians may or should address social issues. Of course we should. Each Christian should take his or her beliefs and values into the public arena and apply them to the important social issues of the day. This is a significant part of kingdom work.

Part of our responsibility as Christians is to exercise our compassion and love for others in tangible ways. Christians should feed the hungry, comfort the sorrowing, and visit the sick. As part of their kingdom service, Christian plumbers plumb since there will not be any leaks in the kingdom. In kingdom service, Christian teachers teach in the sure hope that while now we see darkly, one day we will see face to face, and in that day there won't be any ignorance. As kingdom workers, Christian truckers truck because in the kingdom the good things God has created need to be distributed far and wide.

Also, individual Christians can singly, or through Christian organizations, address the government for solutions to problems that are within the government's proper sphere. One of the simplest ways we in the West carry out this responsibility is to vote for those persons whom we believe will address the problems of the day effectively. Working through Christian organizations, such as Bread for the World or the Center for Public Justice, Christians attempt to influence government policies for the good. Christians are called to be responsible, compassionate, law-abiding citizens.

But these are our responsibilities as individual Christians, or as groups of Christians, and they are all kingdom responsibilities. As each of us carry out his or her civic responsibility before God, it is extremely important that we not confuse what we are saying and doing with church work, for reasons that I will shortly make clear.

The Church's Involvement in Society

Now I will turn to the issue of the institutional church and social justice, which is the main issue of this article.

The primary work of the institutional church is not to promote social justice, it is to warn people of divine justice. Its primary business is not to call society to be more righteous but to tell persons of the righteousness of God in Jesus Christ. Its primary work is not to tell us who to elect to public office, it is to tell those in every nation of the One who elected many for eternal life. The primary work of the institutional church is to open and close the kingdom of God and to nurture the Christian faith. This it does primarily through the pure preaching of the gospel, the pure administration of the sacraments, and the exercise of church discipline.

This is not to say that the institutional church should *never* promote social justice or speak out on behalf of the victims of injustice. There are times during which the institutional church must speak out about social injustices. The institutional church should articulate, in broad terms, the proper goals that social policy should promote. For example, the church should speak out and work for a society that protects all its citizens against acts of violence.

But normally, the church should not take it upon itself to entertain the political question of *how* a particular society can best achieve this goal. That is, the institutional church should, in general, avoid policy statements. Regarding social violence, is gun control a good idea, or will it simply arm only criminals? Are more police officers the best idea, or bigger jails, or mandatory sentences, or some combination of these? The truth is that these are questions that are beyond the institutional church's expertise as a church.

My view is that the institutional church should speak out against preventable poverty but, in most cases, must not recommend exactly which social policies will best reduce poverty. For example, what kind of public assistance, if any, is best, or is private welfare the better option? This is a question that the institutional church as such is not in a privileged position to answer. No doubt individual Christians have their opinions, but I believe that it is taking the Lord's name in vain to claim divine status for your political judgment.

If I decide to vote for some particular political candidate, then that is my decision before God, and I am accountable to him for it. But it is quite a different thing for the council of a congregation to tell its members that voting for that candidate is the Christian choice. If I protest the new welfare rules and write a letter to my congressman with reasons why they are unwise, then that is my decision before God and I am accountable to God for it. But it is a quite different thing for me as a pastor to preach in a sermon that the church stands opposed to welfare reform.

So, the institutional church may outline the broad goals or ends of social policy but normally should not endorse specific policy proposals. However, on some occasions, the church should speak out against a particular social policy. It should do so when the policy is clearly immoral. A policy can be immoral either because the goal of the policy is evil, as in the case of ethnic cleansing, or because the policy is itself immoral, although the goal is morally desirable. Legalized abortion may be one way the government hopes to reduce poverty, a worthy intent, but the church ought to oppose abortion and speak out against it. And so it has. The Christian Reformed Church through its synod has officially spoken out against legalized abortion on several occasions.

It is my opinion that when a synod, rather than some denominational committee or worker, speaks out against some social injustice, it helps guarantee that the specific policy is *clearly* immoral. I do not mean, of course, that moral truth is decided by majority vote. My claim is not ontological. Rather, it is merely epistemological: A significant difference of opinion among Reformed Christians regarding a policy issue is evidence that the morality of the issue is not clear.

Two Dangers

Now consider the two dangers the church must avoid if it tries to address all and only clearly immoral social policies. The first is that it will fail to address all the clearly immoral policies, and so will be silent when it should speak out. In South Africa, some churches failed to speak out against the clearly immoral policy of apartheid. A second, even worse danger, is that a church will speak out and defend the wrong side of the moral issue. When this happens, the church is complicit in the injustice, as happened in some U.S. churches who opposed civil rights for African-Americans.

The church *is* in a privileged position with respect to knowing what is clearly morally permissible and what is morally impermissible, for it has God's written Word. Thus, it should speak out on the clear moral injustices of the day. The truth is, however, that most political issues, in the Western world at any rate, are debates between two or three morally permissible policy options. Choosing among such options requires a kind of worldly wisdom to which Christians as such have no special claim.

Finally, let me give one more reason why the institutional church should be reluctant to enter into the political and social arguments of the day. The reason is this: It tends to compromise the primary work of the church. It does so in two ways. First, it saps energy and resources out of the primary work. Second, it creates a mental association between the institutional church and some political agenda. There are churches that I would not consider attending on a regular basis, not necessarily because their theology is mistaken, but because I associate them with a political agenda with which I personally take issue. To link the cause of Christ with specific social policies that are not morally obligatory seriously impedes the primary work of the church. For these reasons we ought to resist the temptation to use the institutional church as a mouthpiece for our political convictions.

Summary

First, individual Christians are called to be responsible, compassionate, law-abiding citizens.

Second, the institutional church should speak out on the general goals that a society should pursue. It should speak out when the social goals being pursued are evil, as with so-called ethnic cleansing. It should speak out against clearly immoral policies even when they are intended to achieve morally acceptable ends.

However, with respect to the vast majority of political options (whether for or against certain social policies or for or against certain political candidates), the institutional church should keep quiet. It has no privileged knowledge that allows it to choose between these, and, when it does so anyway, it impedes the accomplishing of the primary mission of the institutional church.

Finally, on those clearly moral matters when the church should address a social problem or policy proposal, the church should do so officially in and through its ecclesiastical assemblies. When the issue that must be addressed is national or international, it should be addressed through Synod, not through the denominational board of trustees or some office in the denominational building.

Eight

THE CHURCH
AND SOCIAL JUSTICE*

Peter Vander Meulen

I have spent most of my working life with the Christian Reformed World Relief Committee (CRWRC) in positions overseas—Bangladesh, the Dominican Republic, West Africa—and from that perspective, I want to reflect on the world of the poor in the light of my Reformed heritage and my relationship to Christ.

Assumptions

I want to start by making explicit seven key assumptions on which I base my thesis:

1. The basic tenets of Reformed doctrine are given and are more or less commonly understood.

2. The gospel is truly holistic and conveys a saving, reconciling grace not just for human souls but indeed for ourselves as integral beings—indeed, for all of creation itself.

---

* This essay used with permission here originally appeared as Peter Vander Meulen, "The Church and Social Justice," *Calvin Theological Journal* 34 (1999): 202–6.

3. All of God's created images are entitled to respect and to dignity—all creation groans for a restored relationship with its creator—whether it acknowledges that or not.

4. The church of Christ lives out a paradox: We are called out of the world even as we are called to be *in* the world.

5. The Bible, and Christ in his ministry, repeatedly holds up the poor and those the world considers of no account as having great value. And he explicitly holds them up as his surrogates among us now, and as having a claim upon us because of his care for them.

6. Even as good progress has been made in overcoming hunger and poverty in some parts of the world, any hunger and misery in a world with sufficient food for all is a scandal.

7. Although we have done much in ministry, we have not stretched ourselves out of our areas of comfort and security to meet the poor at their points of pain and poverty. We are really good at relief but less good at personal involvement and scared to death of advocacy; of standing up for the poor and powerless.

Thesis

Now in the light of these assumptions I propose the following thesis:

> The institutional church needs to vigorously encourage—at personal and corporate levels (that is to say congregational, classical, denominational, and ecumenical levels)—faithfulness in doing justice. This need for faithfulness applies to our own personal and corporate (church) affairs as well as personal and church witness in the public square.

By faithfulness in doing justice I mean at least the following three things—in practice. First, identification—be sensitive to injustices that affect those who are poor and powerless. Second, encouragement—promote informed, inclusive, and lovingly tenacious discussion of these issues within our church. In other words, the church should be a community of moral discourse. Third, engagement—change our own behavior. Engage in direct action ministry. Be advocates for and with those who are disenfranchised. Raise these issues in the public square.

To put this more succinctly: Witnessing to issues of justice needs to be an integral part of our Christian Reformed corporate ministry. Some examples of these areas for witness are: life issues, such as euthanasia, abortion, and assisted suicide; wealth and poverty issues, such as the apparent inability of our global economy to sustain vast numbers of people while keeping others in luxury; racism and sexism issues; and stewardship issues, including the care for God's earth.

Why

Why should the church, the CRC, renew and expand its involvement in reflecting on, acting on, and speaking on issues of injustice? I want to make clear that this is no new thing in the CRC that I am arguing for but rather a dramatic increase in the exposure and emphasis that we give to this area. I'm going to present a number of reasons. Further, I suggest that when taken together, they must *convict us* of our need to act. In reflecting on the reasons why, we must consider motive, opportunity, record, and complicity.

Motive

The integrity of the gospel requires holistic (integral) ministry. The gospel message is an integral one. Ministry is essentially holistic. That, I believe, is a given. If the church is properly engaged in ministry, it must also be engaged in public witness against those things that threaten, deny, nullify, or give the lie to that message. Once committed to ministry, we must be committed all the way.

Opportunity

Rarely in history has the North American church, specifically, been in such a position to effectively engage in such witness. This is true, first, because we have unprecedented knowledge about global conditions. We are aware. Second, the (largely Christian) West is in a position to influence the global economy and global affairs as never before. The levers of power are in our hands. Third, because of the stunning advances in global communications, the Christian church, if it chooses, can transcend the barriers of distance, class, ethnicity, and culture and be truly inclusive in its discussions, decision making, and ministry.

Record

The church has always been a force for social transformation, and it has been an advocate for the poor and powerless. From the earliest days of the Christian church, both the ordering of the church and its witness to the proper ordering of society has flowed from the incredible news that the Creator has redeemed his creation. The church has been called out of the world to be a channel of transforming grace. We are called to be in the world but not of it.

I submit that, with all sorts of notable lapses and exceptions, the Christian church has indeed been a channel for transformation and change in culture and society. God gives society good gifts through his church. Indeed the church and its members have been salt and light in this world. Bearing witness and going into action against injustice is nothing new for the church. It is an ancient and honorable thing!

Complicity

The institutional church is implicated in societal and structural injustice. The church exists as a social entity. We take up institutional space. We are not some sort of ethereal body deciding whether or not to stand for justice. We are full and active participants and beneficiaries in systems that we also help to perpetuate. We are, wittingly or unwittingly, part of whatever has gone wrong. We must then also be institutionally active to begin to understand, undo, and restore.

Even if we could avoid this complicity, the church could be an accessory after the fact. To keep quiet is to speak volumes. I suggest that the absence of action and public witness or advocacy is not a neutral "safe" course of action. Silence and inaction are strong messages. Often we say a great deal by saying nothing. And so those of us looking for safe, neutral ground will not find it in silence.

How

But do we have the means by which to address social issues? Do we have the capabilities to deal with significant but complex issues that continually come at us from all directions? Yes, there is a great deal that we can do. Here, I present eight how-tos.

First, we can promote regular and serious analytical work on issues of social justice from our institutions of higher education. This of course is already being done to an extent, but not always in an accessible, timely, and helpful fashion.

Second, the Christian Reformed Church has made major strides in service learning for its youth. We need to consider periodic "in-service learning" for denominational and congregational leadership as well.

Third, similar to service learning is an increase in CRC members who are involved in some form of ministry outside their normal boundaries. Adults are most open to learning when stretched and puzzled by new experiences. To act, reflect on, discuss, and pray about new experiences is to be open to learning and change.

Fourth, we need to increase our value on narrative. Paying attention to stories illustrating God's acts in our lives—both personal and corporate—builds identity in being God's people. It's important that these stories be more than just our own and those like ours. Our attention needs to include a wide spectrum of people. We need to be reminded of the true breadth of the family of God.

Fifth, there is no necessary link between being active in ministry and making changes in our ideas and behavior—growing and maturing. We need to develop materials and opportunities that guide and encourage reflection on the action ministries in which we are involved.

Sixth, advocacy for those who are poor and powerless is an important, legitimate ministry. We need to acknowledge this as a community of faith, celebrate it, and encourage small groups called to advocacy and justice ministry to be salt and light within their congregations.

Seventh, we can develop an action agenda for advocacy in the public square on which the entire denomination can basically agree and on which it can work.

Eighth, we need to encourage the formation of support and discussion groups for members striving to do justice in their vocations and callings.

Conclusion

Just as silence can speak volumes, so, too, can speaking volumes result in saying nothing. We need to avoid the trap of having prophetic words on every issue in the public square.

It is time also to throw out the idea that we should all try to force each other to think exactly alike on things. Groups within the church—with the blessing of the church—can and should take up issues with which they are called and competent to deal. They should be salt and light both within the church and without.

There are times when the institutional church must come to official grips with an issue of great moral or ethical significance. Practically speaking, it seems to make good sense to speak loudly and clearly on things about which we have broad agreement while speaking softly, tentatively, or only to ourselves on things about which we have little agreement.

In summary, whether or not to witness in the public square on matters of justice is not really a choice we have. We are doing so simply by existing as an institution. We are called to fight injustice on the basis of our obedience to the gospel message. It is urgent that we do so because people are suffering and we are able.

Nine

WHY THE CHURCH
MUST NOT STAY SILENT

Liturgy and the Legacy of Colonialism

Mike Hogeterp

S ilence is as powerful a statement as words spoken. When
silence is preparation for careful action, it can lend strength
to the pursuit of truth and justice. In a world that is deepening
in complexity and confusion, we could use more silent reflection
on the good gifts of God and our responsibilities to each other
and to creation itself. Silence can be preparation for liturgy, an
essential and audible action of the church in Sunday services
and in day-to-day ministry—our Sunday-to-Saturday liturgy.
But silence can also be abdication of a responsibility to speak
or act, and that statement too is a powerful one. As the German
theologian Dietrich Bonhoeffer (1906–1945) once confessed, "We
have been silent witnesses of evil deeds. We have become cun-
ning and learned the arts of obfuscation and equivocal speech.
Experience has rendered us suspicious of human beings, and
often we have failed to speak to them a true and open word."[1]

In the Reformed theological tradition, in which we understand that God is reconciling "all things" (Col. 1:20), silence
on a question that affects our neighbors speaks volumes about

---

1. Dietrich Bonhoeffer, *Letters and Papers from Prison*, ed. Christian
Gremmels et al., trans. Isabel Best et al., *Dietrich Bonhoeffer Works*, vol.
8 (Minneapolis, MN: Fortress, 2010), 52.

gaps between our articulated and lived theologies.[2] The church's liturgy of justice and reconciliation must be rooted, passionate, and sometimes even loud. Is our Sunday-to-Saturday liturgy consistent with the beautiful confessions we make in Sunday liturgies?

The great contemporary Reformed thinker Nicholas Wolterstorff has often said that liturgy is *public service* and that justice and worship are linked.[3] Yes, a worship service is a series of rituals performed in public—this is a common understanding of liturgy. But liturgy is more than Sunday morning service; it is the church's ongoing task of presenting—and being present in— Christ's ministry of reconciling all things. The New Testament term from which we get the word *liturgy* also applies to service or ministry more broadly. In this sense it is even applied to the work of civil government (Rom. 13:4). This Sunday-to-Saturday liturgy is one of justice and reconciliation, one that honors the Old Testament prophets' insistence that the presence of injustice in the land indicates the presence of idolatry and meaningless worship. Therefore, for the integrity of liturgy as public service, the church needs to be vocal and active on matters of justice and reconciliation.

The idolatry and sin behind injustice have both individual and corporate dimensions. And given the collective nature of much injustice it is important to confront those ills corporately. Colonialism in North America is a case in point, and the church has an urgent role in confronting it.

The Truth and Reconciliation Commission of Canada (TRC) has made it clear that the trauma caused by seven generations of Indian residential schools has led to poverty and injustice in Indigenous communities and broken relationships between Indigenous People and Settlers.[4] The causes of this injustice are

2. I'm indebted to my friend and mentor Dr. Terry LeBlanc for the concept of articulated and lived theology.

3. Nicholas Wolterstorff, *Until Justice and Peace Embrace* (Grand Rapids: Eerdmans, 1983).

4. See the TRC Executive Summary at http://www.trc.ca/websites/ trcinstitution/File/2015/Honouring_the_Truth_Reconciling_for_the_Future_ July_23_2015.pdf.

complex and rooted in the five-hundred-year history of colonialism. One of the foundations of colonialism is the presumption of European superiority that was articulated in three papal bulls of the late fifteenth century. Collectively known as the Doctrine of Christian Discovery, these papal declarations gave legal room for Christian European rulers to claim the land of non-Christian non-Europeans and to subdue *pagans and savages* to rule over them.[5] This dehumanization ethic denied the fullness of the *imago Dei* (image of God) in Indigenous Peoples. Indigenous scholars, the UN Permanent Forum on Indigenous Issues, and a wide range of others have traced the impact of the Doctrine of Christian Discovery on settler land acquisition and paternalistic and dehumanizing government policy towards Indigenous People in the Americas. An idolatrous and racist assumption of European superiority is a foundation of five hundred years of colonial oppression of Indigenous Peoples and indicates a wide gap between articulated theologies of *imago Dei* and lived practice.

This history and its contemporary effects require a committed and vocal response of the church for a range of reasons. Since the early days of colonization the church played a role in justifying oppression. In specific cases, such as residential schools, churches were agents of assimilation and *civilization.* In the residential schools, churches worked with government to take away language and culture from generations of Indigenous children, and they did so from a conviction that it was a legitimate Christian mission. The Chief Justice of the Supreme Court of Canada and the Truth and Reconciliation Commission have termed the Indian residential schools a *cultural genocide.* As the Holocaust taught us, the dehumanization of a people group results in attempted genocide. One might hope that churches and their mission agencies did not become participants in a cultural genocide intentionally. However, the persistence of the assumptions of European superiority in the Doctrine of Christian Discovery

---

5. For further exploration of the Doctrine of Christian Discovery, see Literature Review of the Doctrine of Discovery Task Force CRCNA at http://www2.crcna.org/site_uploads/uploads/cpd/Lit%20Review%20final2.pdf. See also the UN Permanent Forum on Indigenous Issues Study on the Doctrine of Discovery at http://www.un.org/esa/socdev/unpfii/documents/2014/3.pdf.

colored the whole of colonial culture including the church itself. As Mark MacDonald, National Indigenous Bishop of the Anglican Church of Canada, puts it: "The Doctrine of Discovery has been the handmaid to the idolatrous assumption that God's presence has been confined to Western Civilization—an idea that has all but destroyed the capacity of the major denominations to grow in Indigenous communities."[6] This long-standing shrouding of the Good News, and the denial of the fullness of the image of God in Indigenous People, should certainly provoke the church to a liturgy of clear, passionate, and audible confession, lament, repentance, and tangible efforts for reconciliation.

This ongoing reconciliation liturgy is certainly more than words and noble sentiment inside a worship service or a Bible study. Repentance requires a turning from the moral wounds of colonialism. In this turning towards shalom the church can come to recognize that it has been missing something: the voices and perspectives of Indigenous People and other marginalized peoples that have not been fully heard in the life of the church or society at large. The fulsome contributions of these precious children of God will enrich our collective lives in a wide range of ways. In the turning, as we learn to share life and liturgy more fully with *all* of our neighbors, we cannot deny or change the past of our broken relationships. However, renewing and reconciling relationships gives us the opportunity to step away from the wounds of colonialism toward justice.

Churches and the prime minister of Canada have offered words of apology and confession to Indigenous People. These words are good symbols that require action. All people are indeed image-bearers—and respecting the *imago Dei* in Indigenous Peoples is a task that requires a Sunday-to-Saturday liturgical commitment. The fact that injustices persist in Indigenous communities indicates that the journey of justice and reconciliation will be long. The unjust legacy of colonialism is related, in part, to Euro-superior idolatry in the church, and persists because of the indifference—willful or not—of Settlers and their govern-

---

6. Mark MacDonald, "The Gospel Comes to North America," *First Peoples Theology Journal* 4, no. 1 (June 2006): 95.

ments. Therefore, out of an interest in the integrity of apologies and confessions, and indeed liturgy, the church must not be silent or fearful in the face of the contemporary injustices of colonialism. Confronting the idolatries of colonialism together, as image-bearers of God, both Indigenous Peoples and Settlers, is critical to our mutual wholeness and the integrity of the church.

Silence is not an option as churches stand with Indigenous People to confront the legacy of colonialism. But boisterous and thoughtless action is not appropriate either. The Euro-superior attitude of colonialism assumed that Settlers knew better and could help Indigenous People escape *paganism* and *inferior* ways of living. A majority-euro-church must not, out of guilt for the sins of colonialism, rush in and *fix* the problem by its own design. Listening, learning, and relationships are critical first dispositions.

Early on in our contemporary denominational journey with Indigenous issues, an Indigineous church leader asked why we were interested. The response was the common social justice earnestness: "We want to be a voice for the voiceless," to which the Indigenous leader responded: "With respect, I'm not voiceless; you are deaf." Indigenous People and cultures are resilient in the face of five hundred years of oppression and have rich perspectives on the needs of their communities *and* on our collective lives. Settlers need to recover their hearing of these precious voices in the interest of justice in Indigenous communities and reconciliation between Indigenous People and Settlers.

Listening to the voices of Indigenous People includes efforts to understand the history and legacy of colonialism from the perspective of Indigenous Peoples. The church I serve is doing this through reflection on the Doctrine of Christian Discovery, and the Blanket Exercise,[7] an interactive experience of the history of Indigenous-Settler relations from Indigenous perspective. Knowing the history of oppression and cultural genocide helps us to understand their contemporary legacies: intergenerational trauma, poverty, and chronic marginalization in society and government policy. We must not silence or bury these realities with

---

7. See http://www.crcna.org/BlanketExercise.

obfuscation and equivocal speech, such as the flippant comment "it's in the past, get over it." The colonial past is with us in real and disturbing ways.

Respectful listening and learning about the historic and contemporary realities of Indigenous People can convict us of injustice and the broken relationships between neighbors. Addressing this brokenness starts in relationships—in knowing and honoring the stories of struggle, resilience, and strength of our Indigenous neighbors. And to begin relationships, Settlers can take simple steps: visit a cultural or friendship center or connect with a church in an Indigenous community—all with a learning disposition.[8] Through persistence we can learn and come to know our Indigenous neighbors. And by knowing each other, and listening to our neighbors' concerns, together we can raise a loud voice for justice and reconciliation.

This shared liturgy—of reconciling all things—is urgent for the church in North America. Our silence and complicity in the moral wounds of colonialism, made manifest by the idolatry of Euro-superiority, require a liturgy of confession, lament, learning, relationship building, and justice-seeking with our Indigenous neighbors. For the church in the purported *post-colonial era*, silence and inaction are not options.

---

8. See Steve Corbett and Brian Fikkert, *When Helping Hurts* (Chicago: Moody, 2009), for pointers on the learning disposition.

PART 4

THE CHURCH AND SOCIETY

Ten

DOING SOCIAL JUSTICE

What We Learn from the Practice
of the North American Church

Kevin R. den Dulk

T he problem of religious persecution is both global and growing. The unrelenting reports of the suffering of the faithful
are no less horrifying for their familiarity. It is difficult to imagine
an injustice that cries out more urgently for a Christian response.
Persecution is a violation of shalom, a breaking of God's purposes
for human relationships.

But does a Christian obligation to confront persecution mean
the *church* ought to act? One argument for the church's engagement could be framed this way: Churches are comprised of
Christians. If Christians have an obligation to respond to persecution, then the churches they comprise have that obligation,
too. But this argument is obviously fallacious. We often have
responsibilities as individuals that we do not necessarily place
on organizations that hold our membership. I have an obligation
to raise my children, but I certainly do not expect my bank to
have the same obligation.

To put the point a different way: The church as an institution
is not merely an aggregation of the interests and obligations
of its members. The church, as God's gift of community to his
people, has its own distinctive purposes. So how we describe the
role of the church in addressing an injustice such as persecution

depends on how we understand the church's purposes. Do those purposes encompass "doing justice" (see Micah 6:8)? If so, how? These are indeed controversial and complex questions.

Social Justice and the Practices of the Church

This volume includes many reflections on these questions that take Reformed theology as a starting point. I accept that theology, but I am only a dabbler in the theological arts. Rather than starting with theology, my approach to the church and justice starts with empirical observation. What do we learn about the responsibility of the church to do justice by examining the actual practices of churches?

Consider again the example of religious persecution. Some colleagues and I recently completed an extensive study, commissioned by the Christian Reformed Church in North America on behalf of its member churches, about the problem of persecution and its relation to religious liberty.[1] Our mandate included two key elements: (1) craft a theological framework for understanding "the injustice of religious persecution"; and (2) "propose individual and group action that empowers the [North American] church … to walk alongside and intercede on behalf of those who are subject to religious persecution." Note that these elements of the mandate assume that the church not only has a role in framing instances of injustice, but also should take action *as the church* to confront those injustices.

One might interpret "church" in the second part of the mandate in the general sense of the body of all believers—what some in the Reformed tradition call the church as organism, which is to be distinguished from the church as institution. Several chapters in this volume develop that distinction more fully. But the fact is that the denominational mandate was intended in large part for the church as institution. Leaders asked for our com-

---

1. Committee to Study Religious Persecution and Liberty, "Final Report," in *Agenda for Synod 2016* (Grand Rapids: Christian Reformed Church, 2016). See also Kevin R. den Dulk and Robert J. Joustra, *The Church and Religious Persecution* (Grand Rapids: Calvin College Press, 2015).

mittee's proposals to guide offices within the denomination that are tasked with either equipping member churches directly or acting on their behalf.

One of these agencies within the Christian Reformed Church explicitly signals a denominational priority: the Office of Social Justice. It is worth dwelling on that priority, because many denominations across North America have embraced the idea that the institutional church is an agent of a distinctively "social" type of justice. The Episcopal Church, United Church of Canada, National Baptist Convention of America, and Presbyterian Church (USA) have prominent offices with "social justice" in their names.[2] The conferences of Catholic bishops in both Canada and the United States shape their public witness around the Vatican's statements on social justice.[3] The National Baptist Convention (USA) integrates a focus on social justice directly into its mission statement.[4] The AME Church, Anglican Church of Canada, Evangelical Lutheran Church in America, and numerous others have public declarations that attest to their commitment to social justice or "justice for society."

Perhaps these messages about social justice give us some insight into the appropriate role of the church in doing justice. But what do these denominational uses of the concept of social justice really entail?

A first answer could simply treat social justice as a meaningless and unhelpful concept. After all, in a strict sense of the term *justice*, it is redundant to use the adjective *social*. Justice is always social—or, more precisely, *relational*. The oldest definitions of justice—"to give what is due," for example—assume that justice

---

2. The Social Justice and Advocacy Engagement Office, Community and Social Justice Ministries, the Commission on Social Justice, and the Committee on Social Justice, respectively.

3. The US Conference of Catholic Bishops has excerpted those statements here: http://www.usccb.org/issues-and-action/human-life-and-dignity/vatican-statements-on-social-justice.cfm. They are generally applications of the church's explicit teaching in an article of part 3 of its Catechism, titled "Social Justice," http://www.vatican.va/archive/ccc_css/archive/catechism/p3s1c2a3.htm.

4. See http://www.nationalbaptist.com/about-us/mission--objectives.html.

has subjects and objects, agents and recipients. Pick a good that is in some way distributed in society: wealth, the right to vote, education, or the freedom to practice religion. If person X is due that good, then some other entity Y has an obligation to help X secure that good. To be sure, different theories of justice suggest different sets of obligations between X and Y. A socialist sees a role for robust government in redistributing wealth to satisfy (at minimum) the basic needs of citizens, while the ardent libertarian envisions government as playing a minimal part in the distribution of wealth, primarily by protecting freely contracting parties from force or fraud. Yet both the socialist and libertarian define a social relationship between the individual and the state that seeks to ensure that people receive what is due, that they are treated justly. On this account, then, to say that justice is social is simply to reinforce an essential part of its definition—to name the relationship between X and Y—and therefore to add little meaning to the concept.

But the Christian churches that speak the language of social justice appear to attribute a stronger meaning to the word *social*. They do not see it as redundant and irrelevant. For some, social justice is distinguished by *specific* goods in society that have a special scriptural resonance. A high-profile example is recent public discussions about income and wealth. The Bible speaks extensively about poverty, often in terms of justice, so today many churches have concluded that they ought to focus on the poor and economic inequality. But there are countless other social goods, and the denominations I noted earlier have articulated a biblical warrant for tackling injustice related to a large number of them. Here is a selected inventory: immigration and mobility, the health of the climate and environment more generally, due process in court, equitable treatment of released prisoners, equal opportunities across racial groups or genders, freedom of religion, freedom from violence, dignity in old age, healthcare, access to housing, and the humane treatment of livestock.

There is no doubt that these are all worthy concerns. But if our goal is greater clarity about the role of the church in doing justice, the focus on these social goods does not get us very far. It is difficult to extract a coherent understanding of social justice from a range of goods that is so capacious. And even if we could identify a coherent set of themes in this list of goods, we are still left with the problem that the goods themselves are examples of social justice, not definitions of what social justice is and what churches have to do with it. These examples suggest *what* goods might fit within a definition, but not *why* they belong there.

But perhaps *social* has a different referent for many churches: not as the kind of goods that society distributes, but rather as the kind of institutions that help secure those goods. The late philosopher John Rawls, for example, famously said that justice is "the first virtue of social institutions." While Rawls is not exclusive here—he does not argue that justice is *only* a quality of social institutions, or that social institutions *only* focus on justice—he nevertheless suggests that there is a set of "social" institutions whose principal priority is to do justice. Indeed, that is precisely how Rawls goes on to characterize the principles of what he calls "social justice": they "provide a way of assigning rights and duties in the basic institutions of society and they define the appropriate distribution of the benefits and burdens of social cooperation."[5]

Rawls' conception of justice is quite complex, and it generated a cottage industry of philosophical inquiry and critique that I will avoid here. But it is worth noting a couple of points: Rawls generally saw the state as the key social institution in his theory, and the primary focus of the state—social justice—as the distribution of goods that serves the least advantaged in society. While many churches endorse Rawls' focus on the least advantaged, they rarely talk about social institutions in this limited way. The state matters, to be sure, but most Christian denominations see a central place for civil society—families, schools, labor unions, other voluntary associations, and houses of worship themselves—in doing social justice as well. Still, the idea that institutions—whether the state or those in civil society—are *agents* of social justice resonates deeply within many

---

5. John Rawls, *A Theory of Justice* (Cambridge, MA: Harvard University Press, 1971), 3–4.

Christian traditions, most notably Reformed Protestantism and Roman Catholicism.[6]

But defining social justice in terms of its agents is no more clarifying than defining it in terms of social goods. One reason is a slipperiness in thinking about who ought to advance what kind of justice. Some Reformed thinkers, for example, prefer to speak of the work of the state as a form of *public* justice, not social justice. The distinction between public and social justice matters because it implies that the state has a unique responsibility to use law and regulation to ensure that justice reigns more generally in society.[7] Civil society does not have the same law-making or law-implementing function. But there is an even more basic definitional problem: To identify agents of social justice is not to define social justice. To suggest *who* should advance social justice does not tell us what social justice is.

A third strategy for conceptualizing social justice focuses less on *what* goods are distributed or *who* is distributing those goods and more on *why* we distribute goods in the first place. From this perspective, the social part of social justice reflects a vision of the good society, of a society organized such that human beings can live together in peace and even joy. Specific institutions in society help secure specific social goods *because* God created human beings to live in a specific kind of relationship. This vision

---

6. For recent discussions about the role of faith-based organizations in the pursuit of justice, see Stephen V. Monsma, *Pluralism and Freedom: Faith-Based Organizations in a Democratic Society* (Lanham, MD: Rowman and Littlefield, 2012) and Stephen V. Monsma and Stanley W. Carlson-Thies, *Free to Serve: Protecting the Religious Freedom of Faith-Based Organizations* (Grand Rapids: Brazos, 2015).

7. See, for example, chapter 9 of Davis T. Koyzis, *Political Visions and Illusions: A Survey and Christian Critique of Contemporary Ideologies* (Downers Grove, IL: IVP Academic, 2003). The name of the Center for Public Justice, a think tank with roots in Reformed thinking on politics and policy, illustrates the point. See the contribution of Stephanie Summers, CPJ's Executive Director, in this volume.

can come in different forms,[8] but they share the insight that we cannot do justice—we cannot give human beings their due—unless we give an account of why they are deserving.

As a way of understanding social justice, this focus on the grounds for justice is a more compelling approach than the alternatives. And most denominations in North America do embrace—or at least gesture toward—this approach. The Christian Reformed Church's Office of Social Justice, for example, describes social justice as "God's original intention for human society: a world where ... peace (shalom) reigns."[9] Many others invoke some notion of the common good and love of neighbor (especially emphasized among Roman Catholics), or that human beings, as image-bearers of God, are created for relationships that call forth love and mercy, or some combination of notions.

Social Justice and the Moral Authority of the Church

But to return to a variation on our question: Do these churches' grounds for social justice help us understand the role churches ought to play, if any, in doing justice? It is not always clear that they do—and that is perhaps because, in the final analysis, we are simply asking the wrong question. To understand the role of the church, it is not enough to point out that important goods are poorly distributed in society, or that institutions in general have a role to play in addressing the distribution of goods, or that God has created us to seek basic goods in relationship with others. We still need an account of how the church as an institution—not

---

8. There are too many examples to rehearse here. For an illustration of a rigorous philosophical perspective, see Nicholas Wolterstorff, *Justice: Rights and Wrongs* (Princeton: Princeton University Press, 2008). For more accessible discussions from different Christian traditions, see Timothy Keller, *Generous Justice: How God's Grace Makes Us Just* (New York: Dutton, 2010) and Ronald Sider, *Just Politics: A Guide for Christian Engagement* (Grand Rapids: Brazos, 2012).

9. Christian Reformed Church Office of Social Justice, "Why Social Justice?" http:// www.crcna.org/pages/osj_socialjustice.cfm.

as a group of individuals who might want to do something about a moral outrage—ought to act on social justice.

Again, I am not a theologian, but perhaps again the empirical observations of social science might point us in a helpful direction.

When the church speaks to questions of justice, it seeks to *influence* a response. Hence a reasonable question might be: When is the church as an institution most influential? Or the converse: When is it the least? Recent scholarly work on the church suggests that its cultural influence in North America is waning.[10] A commonly cited factor in this decline is the church's role in politics. In fact, some social scientists, pointing to data on declining membership, have suggested that the efforts by churches to enter the practical work of politics—lobbying, advocacy for specific bills, electoral activity—have backfired for a key aspect of their mission: bringing people together in a community of believers.[11]

These claims are nothing new. Alexis de Tocqueville, the French observer of North American society in the early nineteenth century, marveled at the political relevance of churches in the young United States. But he noted a counterintuitive dynamic: churches seemed to have greatest influence when they were perceived as *least* political.[12] Their power came from their moral authority, and moral authority would diminish if clergy had strong partisan associations. After all, party factions are temporary, fractious, and tied to special interest. In contrast, the claims of the church as a moral community are timeless and rooted in the purposes of God.

---

10. For a review of the data and literature, see Pew Research Center, "Nones on the Rise," http://www.pewforum.org/2012/10/09/nones-on-the-rise/#_ftnref10.

11. The most important work in recent years is Robert Putnam and David Campbell, *American Grace: How Religion Divides and Unites Us* (New York: Simon and Schuster, 2010).

12. Tocqueville discusses this phenomenon in a chapter on "The Main Causes which Tend to Maintain a Democratic Republic in the United States," in *Democracy in America*, vol. 1, trans. Gerald Bevan (New York: Penguin, 2003), 399–52.

So does this mean that churches ought not pursue a vision of social justice? Far from it. Churches do have a role as moral protagonists on key issues of the day. The question is not whether, but how. When my colleagues and I were confronted with that question in our study of religious persecution, we answered this way:

> Churches have the greatest influence when their advocacy is strategic, not tactical—that is, when they present a moral vision and communicate the breadth and depth of support for it rather than getting into the nitty-gritty of whom to lobby, where to litigate, or how to craft policy language. Church members as *Christian citizens* can and should be engaged at both the broadest and most specific levels. But churches as *institutions* should ... refrain from the technical and specific work of public policy.[13]

The church ought to pursue the claims of justice. But churches are not interest groups or think tanks or party factions. They have a key role, but that role is limited to use a Reformed inflection—to their own sphere. And it is precisely in those limitations that churches will find their strongest voice.

---

13. See Committee to Study Religious Persecution and Liberty, "Final Report."

Eleven

DISTINCTIVELY CHRISTIAN THINK TANKS

The Practices of Principled Pluralism, Public Justice, and the Church as Organism

Stephanie Summers

W hat is a think tank? These organizations typically conduct research and advocacy concerning public policy. While government think tanks do exist, in the United States and Canada most are nonprofit organizations and receive the majority of their funding from private donors, consulting revenue, and grant funding for research.[1] Most think tanks represent themselves to the public and to government as independent. Yet each comes from a perspective, an animating philosophy—whether that perspective is based on a specific political ideology, shared values, or the promotion of common interests. Sometimes the intersection of funding source and perspective is abundantly clear, but studies of think tanks have generally observed that most are not busy merely crafting the wishes of their funders into specific policy proposals.

---

1. For an overview of think tanks in North America and around the world, see James G. McGann, "2014 Global Go To Think Tank Index Report," University of Pennsylvania Think Tanks and Civil Societies Program, March 1, 2015, http://repository.upenn.edu/cgi/viewcontent.cgi?article=1008&context=think_tanks.

Why are think tanks necessary? At their best, independent think tanks fulfill an important role in political communities. Think tanks explore big ideas about political communities and the role and responsibilities of government and citizens within them. Think tanks examine questions within a specific political community, for example, looking at the health of the relationship of government to civil society institutions. Other think tanks might examine questions of the relationship of nations. Most think tanks seek to apply the implications of their ideas as they develop answers to challenging political questions by advising government officials, or by educating citizens about the well-being of their political communities, or by equipping them to advocate for specific policy proposals.

So, one may ask, why do we need distinctively Christian think tanks? There are at least three common yet wrong ways to answer this question.

The first wrong answer is based on praxis that looks to and seeks to imitate the techniques and aims of other think tanks. Wrong answer number one goes like this: Since think tanks are organizations coming from diverse ideological perspectives seeking to influence the shape of the political community, we need Christian think tanks to participate in the competition of ideas, where the "winner" earns the prize of influencing policymakers.

The second wrong answer is related to the first, and is based on a false understanding of the role of citizens and government in a democratic political community. On this understanding, the high calling of government officials is distorted and debased. Government officials are reduced to mere brokers of the interests of citizens who elected them for the purpose of furthering those interests. So wrong answer number two goes like this: We need Christian think tanks to help Christian citizens represent the interests of Christians before policymakers and to craft and promote policies that reflect Christian interests.

Lastly, the third wrong answer is based on a conflation of the role of the church as institute and the church as organism. Wrong answer number three goes like this: We don't need distinctively Christian think tanks after all. Rather, the Christian faith requires the explicit proclamation of God's Word, and that is the work of the church. Therefore, we need the church to weigh in with its perspective on proposed or current public policies. In this wrong understanding, it is the church, not distinctively Christian think tanks, that must make policy prescriptions that serve to proclaim the implications of the gospel to the unbelieving world. Most often, these church-based proclamations come in the form of specific policy prescriptions accompanied by supportive biblical references. And while this practice itself is not out of step with the practices of think tanks that base their own proclamations on specific canons, it is not the practice itself that is the error.

This wrong answer—that there is no need for distinctively Christian think tanks if the church just does its job—is wrong because it conflates the task of the church as institute and the church as organism. Indeed, the church as institute *and* organism must proclaim the truth of the gospel. But the two should not be conflated. The church as institute bears responsibilities that are distinct from the church as organism. As Jessica Driesenga has articulated, "The church as an institution is gathered around the Word and sacraments; it corresponds to how the church is often identified, that is, by its corporate worship, the offices of the church, the official programs of the church, and administration of the Word and sacrament."[2] God has given to the church as institute an awesome task, one that requires sustained work to develop theological frameworks and articulations of moral doctrine for providing instruction for what it is to live as God's people.

An unintended but serious potential consequence of the church as institute mapping the truth of the gospel to articulated policy prescriptions is that when the church as institute's prescriptions are rejected by a pluralistic society, the validity of the gospel's claims are also rejected. Throughout history there have been times when the political defeat of policy prescriptions articulated by the church as institute have been so scandalous or so spectacular that it has meant that the truth of the gospel was not only rejected by unbelievers, but questioned by the faithful too. Thus it is the work of the church as organism—the communal life of

---

2. See page 46.

believers who carry good news into the world in every vocation, including citizenship—that must animate distinctly Christian think tanks set apart from the church as institute.

Now, leaving the wrong answers aside, there are at least three right answers to the question of why we need distinctively Christian think tanks.

The first right answer is rooted in the reality that we need Christian think tanks organized around an understanding of what it means that human beings are created to bear the image of God, which is the basis of human dignity. Almost every current cultural message equates citizenship, human worth, and human dignity with the maximization of individual autonomy and self-interest. This view is profoundly different than what it is for citizens to bear the image of God.

The focus of Christian think tanks on image-bearing has two major implications. First, simple observation makes clear that being an active citizen is not a solo activity, or a responsibility that only must be taken up when one's individual life or property is endangered. Christian think tanks and the citizens who animate and engage them articulate that image-bearing citizenship is not a solo activity. Christians are indeed called by God to be a body, and this is true with our citizenship. No responsible citizen sits on the sidelines. Christian think tanks articulate that bearing God's image as citizens cannot be done alone: organizing for political service within the political community will lead to Christian think tanks and other organizations where citizens hold differentiated roles, possess various degrees of specialization and expertise, and juggle a diversity of responsibilities at different seasons of life that will allow for more participation at certain times than at others.

This is where the second implication of what it means to bear God's image as citizens comes into view. Embodying this belief in the context of a Christian think tank provides a sharp contrast to institutions that promote the maximization of personal autonomy. Christian think tanks formed for the purpose of supporting the image-bearing vocation of citizenship must also articulate the conclusions reached from the belief that undergirds this view. Since every human being is made to bear the image of God, this has direct policymaking implications for how a Christian think tank must proceed prudentially toward policy prescriptions. Rather than starting from a vantage point that looks at the maximization of personal autonomy or considers only the economic utility of human persons in policymaking, a Christian think tank will build from a starting point that views every human as possessing ontological worth and existing in relationship with others.

The second right answer to why we need distinctively Christian think tanks is rooted in an understanding of God's good creational intent for human development of political community toward human flourishing as our end. This is part of our fulfillment of the cultural mandate. We need Christian think tanks that articulate a normative framework, within which is expressed God's creational intent for the furthering of the institutions of society that lead to human flourishing. These institutions include marriage, family, and church, but also government, as well as institutions that support the vocation of citizenship.

As a distinctively Christian think tank works to ensure justice for all, the scope of its work must include the articulation of the basis for and extent of Christian participation and cooperation in a pluralistic political community, which is called principled pluralism. Human flourishing is an end that is meant not only for Christians, but for our fellow citizens who are avowedly not so, and distinctively Christian think tanks must orient their work toward this end in the political realm.

A distinctively Christian think tank will also develop and articulate public justice as the guiding norm or principle for government, thus helping to clarify that government holds important responsibilities, but that in fulfilling them government must ensure room for other institutions to fulfill their important responsibilities too and must not undercut them intentionally or inadvertently. And a Christian think tank will be concerned with communicating the basis for all this thought and application in such a way that it both inspires and equips citizens to take seriously their responsibilities to shape their political communities for the good of all. As James W. Skillen rightly exhorts,

> Christians therefore should see life in the political com-
> munity as one of the arenas in which they have been called
> to serve in organized ways as stewards of justice and rec-
> onciliation for the sake of all their civic neighbors. Active
> citizenship oriented toward justice for all should be under-
> stood as an integral part of the Christian way of life, lived
> out as an expression of our prayer for God's kingdom to
> come and God's will to be done on earth as it is in heaven.[3]

The third right answer to why we need distinctively Christian think tanks is rooted in an understanding of God's patience in bringing about the consummation of all things in God's time. Throughout successive generations the basis for their work will not change, but Christian think tanks will conduct research and promote conclusions about what changes should be made for the well-being of all persons and institutions within a particular political community in light of the public policy questions faced by citizens of that time, and they will communicate these ideas to policymakers and citizens and attend to the well-being of future citizens and the political community as a whole. We need Christian think tanks, animated and engaged by the church as organism, by citizens, to do this long, hard, slow, obedient, yet always hopeful work in this already-but-not-yet season while God is still patient.

Within this season, we also need distinctively Christian think tanks to protect the work of the church as institute from being rejected outright in a pluralistic society as that society changes. It is the church as organism, the communal life of believers, that carries the implications of the good news into the world. The church as organism is responsible to form distinctively Christian think tanks for the explicit purpose of supporting one of the many vocations of God's people—citizenship. It is these citizens who articulate the implications of the good news for a political community. Distinctively Christian think tanks animated by the church as organism protect the church as institute so that it may fulfill its God-given task.

---

3. James W. Skillen, *The Good of Politics: A Biblical, Historical, and Contemporary Introduction* (Grand Rapids: Baker Academic, 2014), 144.

Twelve

SOCIAL JUSTICE
AND CHRISTIAN OBEDIENCE

Present and Future Challenges

Vincent Bacote

G od's people have never lived in a world free of tension and
opposition. Each era presents unique challenges and contemporary expressions of perennial problems. With no pretense
of comprehensiveness, I suggest some of the challenges today
and (possibly) in the future.

One place to start is with the question of Christian commitment to social justice. Depending upon the denominational backgrounds or streams of tradition (an important factor in light of the
growth of nondenominational churches), the value placed upon
social justice as a legitimate expression of Christian faithfulness
will vary. Today there is less fear than in some times past of an
immanent, this-worldly-oriented social gospel that reduces the
aims of Christianity to building God's kingdom on earth through
various means. And yet there remain numerous Christians who
question the place of social justice as part of Christian mission.

Disputes will continue about the proper understanding of
Christian mission; one way to think about this is to ask which
aspects of Christian doctrine are most prominent. Is mission primarily understood because of the way we interpret the doctrine

of, for instance, creation, church, kingdom, sanctification, or eschatology? Even within the understanding of these doctrines lie important areas of emphasis that can largely influence the way Christians regard the place of social justice in the Christian life and practice, if it has any place at all. For instance, if the church is understood primarily as a community of worship whose witness is primarily the proclamation of Christ's reconciling work, there will not be the same priority given to matters of social justice as there would be where the church is understood as a prophetic and liberation-oriented community that seeks to be agents of change in the pursuit of justice around the world. Sorting out the central theological impetus for the practice of Christian fidelity in the world is a perpetual task for each generation of Christians, and questions of method, focus, and context require thoughtful engagement.

A significant reason this foundational matter will remain challenging is not only the confusion about the reasons to pursue social justice but also ambivalence about the prospects of "success." In the United States many Christians regard the public strategies of the past twenty-five years as largely unfruitful because there have been notable "losses" and because the public posture has yielded a negative public reputation for Christians.[1]

Though this challenge remains, it presents opportunities for reflection that could lead to better theological reasoning for the pursuit of social justice and refined or renewed strategies for addressing the array of cultural, economic, and political concerns.

What are some of the present and future challenges for those who conclude that the pursuit of social justice is proper to Christian engagement in the world? Here is a selection of issues, though hardly exhaustive.

Marriage. While the jury is out regarding the impact of the legalization of same-sex marriage, what seems beyond dispute is that the life outcomes for children raised in single-parent

---

1. For one example, see David Kinnaman and Gabe Lyons, *UnChristian: What a New Generation Really Thinks about Christianity … and Why It Matters* (Grand Rapids: Baker, 2012), which includes survey data on the negative perception of Christians.

households are starker than for children raised in a home where the parents are married.[2] One of the largest challenges here is how to facilitate a culture where marriage and parenting are desirable and understood as more than merely means to personal fulfillment and existential satisfaction. Though this issue is perhaps regarded more as a cultural or political issue, it is a social justice issue because the crisis around marriage has yielded devastation, particularly for those below middle class. The life opportunities are diminished for children born to single parents in poorer demographics.

Religious Liberty. The pursuit of societies that value equality is a high aspiration, but one that has many complications if the concept of equality is not an area of agreement. We now find ourselves in a time of greater religious and worldview pluralism, and societies that wish to recognize and protect rights such as freedom of association and freedom of expression are experiencing a time of great challenge. Matters of religious liberty are one area where challenges will remain for some time. A major question for Christians concerns the way that they wish to pursue religious liberty. Is the religious liberty in question only for Christians or for all forms of religion? Do we desire a society that allows religious persons and institutions the freedom to worship and the full exercise of their beliefs, even if this means that in some cases religious persons and institutions may deny membership or the offer of services to some persons because of conflicts with their own beliefs and religious practices? This challenge requires the best political and legal minds, and may require strategies where there is compromise across great differences in perspective. Christians with differences of conviction about such a possible compromise must come together to propose and pursue a winsome strategy.

Race. Human conflicts and systems of oppression stemming from differences in ethnic identity is as old as the early chapters

---

2. See "Social Indicators of Marital Health & Well-Being: Trends of the Past Five Decades," in *The State of Our Unions* (Charlottesville, VA: National Marriage Project and Institute for American Values, 2012), 89–96, http://www.stateofourunions.org/2012/social_indicators.php#families.

of Genesis; in recent centuries one of the most virulent forms has
been connected to what we call "race" (an inadequate classifica-
tion scheme), particularly as connected to matters such as the
legacy of chattel slavery and Jim Crow laws in the United States.
Few would dispute that matters related to race have improved
in recent decades, but in the United States and beyond there are
numerous reminders that considerable difficulties remain. In the
church, one of biggest challenges is how to talk about questions
of race, as some tend to emphasize individual expressions of
racial prejudice and conflict while others emphasize corporate
and systemic factors that continue to disadvantage minorities.
In order to move forward it will require a commitment to enter
into conversations where the complexities are acknowledged
(resisting simplistic reductions to either individual or systemic
causes) and multiple strategies are pursued. The latter requires
addressing the challenge of how to speak about racial concerns as
part of the task of Christian ethics. (Try this exercise sometime:
survey the number of texts on Christian ethics that address race.
Spoiler: it is a low number.[3]) Though this is a difficult challenge,
it is also one of the best opportunities for a Christian witness that
models how people can live together and seek mutual flourishing
across ethnic and racial divides.

Gender. Around the world, the prospects of flourishing
for girls and women remain a topic of concern. While in some
Christian settings this topic is focused on the participation of
women in church leadership (ordination, preaching, and so on),
there are questions of women's access to education and public
health, particularly in societies where it may be dangerous for
women to seek the kinds of flourishing that seems typical for
many in the modern West. Among the complexities in this domain
are the challenges of navigating contextual and cultural norms.
One notable example may suffice: female circumcision or genital
mutilation (and health concerns precipitated by the procedure)

---

3. Glen H. Stassen and David P. Gushee, *Kingdom Ethics: Following
Jesus in a Contemporary Context* (Downers Grove, IL: IVP Academic,
2003) is one of the exceptions and provides a helpful chapter on the issue
of race (389–408).

has been a matter of concern in the developed world since at least the 1970s and initially seemed to be easy to condemn as a clear instance of female oppression in some Arab and African countries. Today, however, it has become a debated topic (e.g., Is this issue a matter of uniform justice or is the Western condemnation of it a paternalistic practice that actually risks the ostracism of women in their communities?). Perhaps the overall challenge can be framed as follows: if the Christian mission is more than the proclamation of reconciliation with God through Christ and also includes a global witness expressed as the pursuit of justice for all, how do Christians winsomely address complicated challenges that remain for girls and women while properly respecting and dignifying cultures different from our own?

Abortion. What does it mean for Christians to be pro-life? While in the United States the rate of abortion peaked in 1990, each year nearly one million abortions are performed. Here is another way to look at the data: There were nearly fifty-three million legal abortions from 1973 to 2011[4] and there is a striking racial or ethnic component in the United States. As Zoe Dutton writes, "An African-American woman is almost five times likelier to have an abortion than a white woman, and a Latina more than twice as likely, according to the Centers for Disease Control and Prevention."[5] Abortion brings together issues of race, gender, and economics; to address this ongoing challenge will require new strategies that attend to cultural norms and education, and communication strategies that help make clear that those who care about unborn children also care about mothers and recognize the difficulties of women who have unplanned pregnancies (at times the political debate obscures the real persons involved). In

---

4. See "Fact Sheet: Induced Abortion in the United States," Guttmacher Institute, July 2014, https://www.guttmacher.org/pubs/fb_induced_abortion.html.

5. See Zoe Dutton, "Abortion's Racial Gap," *The Atlantic*, September 22, 2014, http://www.theatlantic.com/health/archive/2014/09/abortions-racial-gap/380251/. See also Karen Pazol et al., "Abortion Surveillance— United States, 2006," *Morbidity and Mortality Weekly Report*, Surveillance Summaries, November 27, 2009, http://www.cdc.gov/mmwr/preview/mmwrhtml/ss5808a1.htm?s_cid=ss5808a1_e.

minority communities there is a particular need for a new rhetorical strategy given the association of pro-life concerns with party politics. Some, even many, minorities might say that abortion is a conservative Republican cause espoused by those who advocate for other policies that are seen to be unfriendly to minority communities. While there are certainly exceptions to this perception, many in minority communities—perhaps particularly African-American and Latino—have a political affiliation with groups they perceive to be more favorable to themselves, and these groups are generally pro-choice. Merely to start a conversation on the issue itself requires wading through the connotations that spring from perceived political associations—which is no small task. The numbers alone indicate that this is an issue because human lives are at stake, though it is also a matter of concern because of the way the issue is related to modern cultural norms in a highly sexualized culture.

Environmental Concerns. While debates about climate change continue, environmental concerns of various types remain, such as the effects of waste disposal around the world. Perhaps one of the biggest difficulties here is that concerns about the environment are hardly uniform around the world, and attempts to facilitate common concern among modern and developing nations are fraught with difficulties (e.g., Which countries stand to lose the most economic advantage if such international agreements are reached?). Meanwhile, the need for clean and drinkable water remains (even in some areas of industrialized nations) along with ways to address water and air pollution that comes from processing fossil fuels and manufacturing. Among the biggest challenges is how Christians can attend to these matters first as concerns that stem from a robust theology of creation and second (or even more removed) as political debates. This is difficult because there are many political and economic interests involved. Still, if Christians are to care for the creation as part of the cultural mandate, then environmental issues (especially because of the implications for human flourishing) are not matters to be left to others. Rather than succumbing to simplistic political slogans, difficult work needs to be done when considering contexts such as those where coal is central to the economy. How is one to both take into account the need for economic opportunity, clean air, and water, and the health concerns of many who labor in potentially hazardous conditions? This is a tangled web that we dare not neglect, and it points to the interconnections between environmental and economic issues.

Economic Life and Poverty. Though there has been a recent emergence of books, blogs, and institutions pointing out the connections between Christian faith and the world of business and economics, more attention is needed in this area, particularly in ways that show the connections between fidelity to Christ and attention to economics, business, and work matters. Why is this an issue of social justice? The answer is that issues such as poverty and development (obvious social justice issues in the eyes of many) are intimately connected to questions of economics, business, and work. It may be that the obvious connection to money and wealth creation makes many Christians nervous because of the possibilities of financial idolatry, but this concern should not obscure the fact that one of the most important dimensions of human flourishing is connected to economic life. If Christians are to address poverty by means other than providing aid (not always problematic, but not the best long-term strategy) then it requires considering how to facilitate opportunities for humans to engage in economic activity, which is one mode in which humanity expresses the image of God. To be concerned about poverty is to have a Christian commitment to seeking ways of enabling economic flourishing as a way of providing sustenance and service.

These topics, among others (such as biotechnological challenges, secularism, immigration, criminal justice, and education reform), are areas of life in God's creation where the church can direct its attention and consider paths toward a concrete witness in the present and in the decades ahead. The shape of that witness, and the voices and institutions that sculpt it, are the challenge of our day. The global church, in particular, has pressed questions to North American churches on issues of race, economic justice, and sexuality. Who speaks for churches, and how to speak as the church, as institute or as organism, is a critical question that must be addressed when faced with these enormous challenges. Though debates will ensue about the matters of greatest priority, talk alone will not suffice; it has been time for action ever since God gave humans responsibility for his world.

Historical Epilogue

A CAUTIONARY TALE

Kevin N. Flatt

C ontemporary evangelicals, of course, are not the first
Christians to enter the public square and engage with civil
society in pursuit of social justice. Mainline or liberal Protestants
have long seen the pursuit of social justice as one of their defining
characteristics, and there is much that might be learned from
their experiences over the past several decades. At a minimum,
the way in which at least some mainliners have entered the
arena of social and political activism provides evangelicals with
a cautionary tale.

Consider the case of the United Church of Canada.[1] As most
readers will readily recognize, the United Church's story, *mutatis
mutandis*, is also the story of mainline Protestantism throughout
North America. Formed in 1925 out of a union primarily of leading

---

1. The argument here follows the one I develop in more detail in Kevin
N. Flatt, *After Evangelicalism: The Sixties and the United Church of
Canada* (Montreal and Kingston: McGill-Queen's University Press, 2013).
Another valuable recent source on the history of the United Church in this
period is Phyllis Airhart, *A Church with the Soul of a Nation: Making and
Remaking the United Church of Canada* (Montreal and Kingston: McGill-
Queen's University Press, 2013).

bodies of Presbyterians and Methodists, the United Church has for much of its history been the largest Protestant church in Canada. In the mid-nineteenth century, its Presbyterian and Methodist forebears formed the backbone of Canadian evangelicalism, deeply committed to biblical authority and deathly serious about the proclamation of a gospel of eternal salvation at home and abroad. By the end of the century, however, the assaults of higher biblical criticism, combined with an optimistic Victorian sense of the progress of human knowledge, led the churches' theologians and professors to give up the core tenets of their forefathers' belief system, beginning with the trustworthiness of Scripture and then quickly progressing to hard-to-swallow doctrines like the bodily resurrection of Christ. After a few embarrassing heresy trials involving professors and ministers, both denominations gave up enforcing their doctrinal standards, allowing liberalism to gradually permeate the clergy via the seminaries.

Where did this leave churches whose *raison d'être* had been, more or less, proclaiming the authority of the Bible and the salvation made possible through the resurrection of Jesus Christ? Enter the social gospel. Social activism of various kinds had a long history in evangelicalism, but by making the central purpose of the church the "salvation of society"—the amelioration of social conditions through activism—the social gospel bypassed awkward doctrinal discussions. Preachers could stick to the Sermon on the Mount and selections of the Minor Prophets and avoid theological showdowns with their congregations. Ministers whose theological education had shorn them of belief in original sin or the deity of Christ could still find their purpose in urban planning reform or women's suffrage. Above all, the social gospel allowed the churches to focus on something *practical* and avoid what was often labeled fruitless controversy. The forging of the United Church in 1925 was in large part an attempt to build an organization that could pursue social reform on a national scale—a church defined by its commitment to social justice.

After union, the theological liberalism and social gospel enthusiasm that animated many church leaders penetrated only slowly to the people in the pews. For decades leaders continued to use much of the language and practices of the older evangelicalism, partly because of its power to resonate with the laity, and partly because these themes still resonated with many of the leaders themselves. Gradually, however, liberalism asserted itself, and in the turbulent 1960s the uneasy coexistence between the church's leadership and evangelicalism's legacy came to a decisive end. A new Sunday school curriculum, designed to disabuse lay people of their naïve faith in the reliability of biblical accounts, launched in 1964. New leadership at the church's Board of Evangelism and Social Service decided that social service *is* evangelism, rendering the latter unnecessary. Church leaders developed A New Creed that intentionally omitted liberal stumbling blocks like the Virgin Birth and hell.

At the same time, prominent Canadian journalist Pierre Berton published a book called *The Comfortable Pew*, which castigated the churches for dragging their feet on doctrinal and social issues.[2] The only way churches could survive and remain relevant, claimed Berton, was to jettison outdated doctrinal beliefs while getting out in front of social and political movements like the Sexual Revolution and the New Left. Berton's book galvanized United Church ministers and leaders. In effect, *The Comfortable Pew* became the manifesto of the post-1960s United Church, which succeeded in outpacing public opinion on sexual matters, for example, by pressing for the legalization of abortion in the 1960s, accepting homosexuality in the 1980s, and lobbying for same-sex marriage at the turn of the century. The United Church's economic political prescriptions have also been decidedly left-leaning, stressing themes like increased taxes, central economic planning, and opposition to international trade agreements.

The church also followed the other half of Berton's formula for relevance through its willingness to let go of received Christian doctrines. In one particularly telling example, in 1997 Moderator Bill Phipps, the church's highest elected official, told a major

---

2. Pierre Berton, *The Comfortable Pew: A Critical Look at Christianity and the Religious Establishment in the New Age* (Toronto: McClelland and Stewart, 1965).

newspaper, "I don't believe Jesus was God.... I'm no theologian."[3] When asked if "Jesus is the only way to God," Phipps responded, "No I do not believe that."[4] In response to questions about the historicity of Christ's death and resurrection, Phipps said, "No, I don't believe that in terms of the scientific fact.... I think it's an irrelevant question."[5] The denominational authorities responded by reaffirming his leadership and celebrating the diversity of doctrinal perspectives in the church.

Where has this left the United Church? Politically, it has little of its own to bring to national debates, given the difficulty of distinguishing its positions from those of a host of secular environmentalist and labor groups and the leftward fringe of the New Democratic Party. (Canadian journalists like to call the United Church "the NDP at prayer.") But even if the United Church had something unique to say, it increasingly lacks the numbers and institutional strength to sustain social and political engagement. The denomination is rapidly dwindling and aging, having lost more than half of its membership since the 1960s. Most of its remaining members exhibit low levels of attendance and commitment. *Pace* Bill Phipps and Pierre Berton, it seems that the sorts of people who are interested in joining churches want those churches to have concrete beliefs about things like God, Jesus, and the afterlife. A United Church that will take a firm stance to boycott goods produced by Israeli settlements in the West Bank, but won't rebuke a moderator who denies Christ's deity and resurrection, simply doesn't attract much support *as a church*. Canadians who already think recycling is a good idea, or are suspicious of corporations, or are comfortably agnostic in their religious beliefs, don't need to visit a house of worship on a Sunday morning to be told they're right on all counts. If current trends continue, the United Church, formed to be the social conscience of a nation, will not have any members left to celebrate its 125th birthday.

---

3. "An *Ottawa Citizen* Q&A: Is Jesus God?," in Bill Phipps, *Cause for Hope: Humanity at the Crossroads* (Kelowna, BC: CopperHouse, 2007), 223.

4. "An *Ottawa Citizen* Q&A: Is Jesus God?," 218.

5. "An *Ottawa Citizen* Q&A: Is Jesus God?," 218–19.

What lesson then, is to be drawn from this tale?

Pondering the juxtaposition of the United Church's activism and its numerical collapse, the Canadian news media have sometimes drawn the lesson that religion and politics should be kept separate. Churches have no business meddling in social and political issues, the analysis goes, and if they do, it distracts from their proper concerns. While there is a small kernel of truth to this view, readers of this volume are unlikely to swallow its prescription of social and political quietism. While we need to differentiate carefully between the appropriate social and political roles of the church as organism and the church as institution, there is no realm of human life outside of the authority and care of Jesus Christ.

Others of us may be tempted to conclude that the problem is simply the alignment of the church with the causes of the Left: deep-seated hostility to markets and private enterprise, coupled with naïve faith in state direction of the economy; acquiescence in the disastrous narrative of sexual "liberation"; blindness to the daily slaughter of the unborn; and a fondness for identity politics. This assessment is closer to the mark, since such alignment makes the church a captive of ideological forces that are either only superficially connected to Scripture and the tradition of Christian social thought or entirely foreign to them. But can a similar seduction not also be seen on the Right in churches that uncritically perpetrate nationalism and xenophobia, that shrug off environmental concerns as the province of socialists and pagans, that tacitly bless foreign policies of naked self-interest, that fail to recognize limits to the powers of markets, or that ignore the structural elements of the problem of poverty?

The point here is not to posit some sort of equivalence between Left and Right, or to endorse the one-dimensional political spectrum as the best analytic frame, but rather to point out the danger of well-intentioned activism being taken captive by cultural currents foreign to the gospel. The better lesson to be drawn from the mainline Protestant experience with social activism, then, is this: it is easy for churches to have their activism hijacked by alien ideologies, whether of the Left or of the Right or of some other configuration.[6] To avoid this fate, churches need to cultivate a robust spiritual life and a thoroughly biblical social witness through what might be called a chain of faithfulness:

1. Vibrant, orthodox local churches, willing to reject any gods other than the God of the Bible, shaped by the Word and the sacraments, saturated in prayer, and in general formed by liturgies and practices strong enough to counteract those of the surrounding culture.

2. Trained elders (clergy), including seminary professors and administrators, absolutely faithful to God and their trust, serious about and skilled in the obedient interpretation and exposition of Scripture in communion with the historic and global church, and held accountable by the church.

3. Lay experts, immersed in the life of the church and the teaching of the elders, who can develop, from biblical foundations and the tradition of the church, Christian proposals regarding the pressing social and political issues of the day.

4. Faithful social and political action by the church (institutional and organic, as delineated elsewhere in this volume), guided by the voices of these experts.

The lower links in the chain depend on those above them. A church cannot simply skip to step 4 and expect to do much good. Activism that disregards Scripture or church tradition, or that is not rooted in worship and Word and sacrament, or that does not arise from careful thinking by well-trained Christians knowledgeable in their fields, may be quick and easy, but in the end it will ape culturally dominant patterns of secular activism, and the salt will lose its savor.

---

6. There is a sociological case to be made that the background, education, and work environment of mainline Protestant clergy predispose them to favor the Left, and that the polities of their churches allow them to set the overall political tone, but alas, there is no space to explore these theses here.

To be sure, it is also possible to ignore steps 3 and 4—the error of some conservative evangelicals in the twentieth century. This truncation of the scope of Christian concern is also a serious mistake. But some errors are more fatal than others. The fundamentalists of the 1930s often withdrew from God's call for social engagement, but their children, reading the same Bible whose authority they had defended, rediscovered it. In short, their error was recoverable because they had a reset point. In the case of too many mainline Protestant churches, in contrast, the corrosive influence of theological liberalism progressively undermined the confidence of clergy and laity alike in Scripture and the tradition of the church, leaving no source of truth and authority deeper than the trends of the moment, and ultimately undercutting even their social activism. We would do well not to follow this example. After all, what does it profit a church to pursue social justice, if while doing so it forfeits its soul?

CONTRIBUTORS

VINCENT BACOTE is associate professor of theology and director of the Center for Applied Christian Ethics at Wheaton College. His publications include *The Political Disciple: A Theology of Public Life* and *The Spirit in Public Theology: Appropriating the Legacy of Abraham Kuyper*.

JORDAN J. BALLOR is a research fellow and the executive editor of the *Journal of Markets & Morality* at the Acton Institute for the Study of Religion and Liberty. He is the author and editor of numerous volumes including *Get Your Hands Dirty: Essays in Christian Social Thought (and Action)* and *Ecumenical Babel: Confusing Economics and the Church's Social Witness*. He also serves as a general editor of the Abraham Kuyper Collected Works in Public Theology series.

KEVIN R. DEN DULK holds the Paul B. Henry Chair in Political Science and serves as executive director of the Henry Institute for the Study of Christianity and Politics at Calvin College. He has coauthored or coedited several books, including *Religion and Politics in America, A Disappearing God Gap?, Christianity in Chinese Public Life*, and *The Church and Religious Persecution*.

CONTRIBUTORS

JESSICA DRIESENGA is a doctoral student in Christian ethics at Fuller Theological Seminary in Pasadena, California. Her research and translation work focuses on neo-Calvinist ethics, primarily in the work of Herman Bavinck.

KEVIN N. FLATT is associate professor of history at Redeemer University College in Ancaster, Ontario, where he both serves as director of research and chairs the department of history and international studies. He is the author of *After Evangelicalism: The Sixties and the United Church of Canada* and has published widely on Canadian Protestantism. His work regularly appears in *Comment* and *Faith Today*.

CARL F. H. HENRY (1913–2003) was one of the most important evangelical theologians of the twentieth century. He helped launch the National Association of Evangelicals, was the founding editor of *Christianity Today*, and was a founding faculty member of Fuller Theological Seminary. His many books and articles on Christianity and culture shaped a generation of evangelical thought on the church and social issues.

MIKE HOGETERP directs the Christian Reformed Centre for Public Dialogue, an Ottawa-based justice and reconciliation ministry of the Christian Reformed Church in Canada. He currently chairs the Commission on Justice and Peace of the Canadian Council of Churches and chairs the CRCNA Doctrine of Discovery Task Force.

ROBERT JOUSTRA is director of the Centre for Christian Scholarship and assistant professor of international studies at Redeemer University College in Ancaster, Ontario. He is a coauthor of *How to Survive the Apocalypse: Zombies, Cylons, Faith, and Politics at the End of the World* and *The Church and Religious Persecution*.

DAVID T. KOYZIS is professor of political science at Redeemer University College in Ancaster, Ontario, where he has taught since 1987. He is the author of *Political Visions and Illusions* and, most recently, *We Answer to Another: Authority, Office, and the Image of God*.

118

RICHARD J. MOUW is professor of faith and public life at Fuller Theological Seminary in Pasadena, California, where he served as president from 1993 to 2013. Among his many writings on theology and ethics are *He Shines in All That's Fair* and *Uncommon Decency: Christian Civility in an Uncivil World.* In 2007, Princeton Theological Seminary awarded him the Abraham Kuyper Prize for Excellence in Reformed Theology and Public Life.

J. HOWARD PEW (1882–1971) was cofounder of the Pew Charitable Trusts and chairman of the board of Sun Oil Company. For over thirty years he served as president of the board of trustees of the General Assembly of the United Presbyterian Church in the U.S.A. He also served as chair of the National Lay Committee of the National Council of the Churches of Christ.

STEPHANIE SUMMERS is the CEO of the Center for Public Justice in Washington, DC, and is the publisher of the online journals *Capital Commentary* and *Shared Justice.* She is a coauthor of *Unleashing Opportunity: Why Escaping Poverty Requires a Shared Vision of Justice.*

PETER VANDER MEULEN is coordinator for the Office of Social Justice and Hunger Action of the Christian Reformed Church. Previously, he worked for over twenty years with the Christian Reformed World Relief Committee in Central America, Asia, the Caribbean, and West Africa.

CALVIN P. VAN REKEN is professor of moral theology at Calvin Theological Seminary in Grand Rapids, Michigan, and is an ordained minister in the Christian Reformed Church.

MICHAEL R. WAGENMAN is director of the Kuyper Centre for Emerging Scholars and is Christian Reformed Chaplain at University of Western Ontario in London, Ontario.

Made in the USA
San Bernardino, CA
22 June 2016